ALSO BY TAMARA SHOPSIN

ARBITRARY
STUPID
GOAL

ARBITRARY STUPID GOAL

TAMARA SHOPSIN

 MCD · *Farrar, Straus and Giroux · New York*

MCD

Farrar, Straus and Giroux

18 West 18th Street, New York 10011

Grateful acknowledgment is made for permission to reprint the following material: "Baby," from *The Collected Poems of Langston Hughes* by Langston Hughes, edited by Arnold Rampersad with David Roessel, Associate Editor, copyright © 1994 by the Estate of Langston Hughes. Used by permission of Alfred A. Knopf, an imprint of the Knopf Doubleday Publishing Group, a division of Penguin Random House LLC. All rights reserved.

Owing to limitations of space, illustration credits can be found on page 325.

Library of Congress Cataloging-in-Publication Data
Names: Shopsin, Tamara, author.
Title: Arbitrary stupid goal / Tamara Shopsin.
Description: New York : MCD / Farrar, Straus and Giroux, 2017.
Identifiers: LCCN 2016059399 | ISBN 9780374105860 (hardback) |
   ISBN 9780374715809 (ebook)
Subjects: LCSH: Shopsin, Tamara—Childhood and youth. | Shopsin, Tamara—
   Family. | Greenwich Village (New York, N.Y.)—Biography. | New York (N.Y.)—
   Biography. | Restaurants—New York (State)—New York. | Family-owned
   business enterprises—New York (State)—New York. | Bohemianism—
   New York (State)—New York. | Greenwich Village (New York, N.Y.)—
   Social life and customs. | New York (N.Y.)—Social life and customs. |
   BISAC: BIOGRAPHY & AUTOBIOGRAPHY / Artists, Architects,
   Photographers. | BIOGRAPHY & AUTOBIOGRAPHY / Women.
Classification: LCC F128.68.G8 S56 2017 | DDC 974.7/1043092 [B]—dc23
LC record available at https://lccn.loc.gov/2016059399

Designed by Tamara Shopsin

Our books may be purchased in bulk for promotional, educational, or business use. Please contact your local bookseller or the Macmillan Corporate and Premium Sales Department at 1-800-221-7945, extension 5442, or by e-mail at MacmillanSpecialMarkets@macmillan.com.

www.fsgbooks.com • www.mcdbooks.com
www.twitter.com/mcdbooks • www.facebook.com/mcdbooks

1   3   5   7   9   10   8   6   4   2

This is a work of nonfiction. However, the names and identifying characteristics of certain individuals have been changed to protect their privacy.

For my mom & the Wolfawitzes

CONTENTS

ARBITRARY
STUPID
GOAL

A SYMPHONY

The imaginary horizontal lines that circle the earth make sense. Our equator is 0°, the North and South Poles are 90°. Latitude's order is airtight with clear and elegant motives. The earth has a top and a bottom. Longitude is another story. There isn't a left and right to earth. Any line could have been called 0°. But Greenwich got first dibs on the prime meridian and as a result the world set clocks and ships by a British resort town that lies outside London.

It was an arbitrary choice that became the basis for precision. My father knew a family named Wolfawitz who wanted to go on vacation but didn't know where.

It hit them. Take a two-week road trip driving to as many towns, parks, and counties as they could that contained their last name: Wolfpoint, Wolfville, Wolf Lake, etc.

They read up and found things to do on the way to these Wolf spots: a hotel in a railroad car, an Alpine slide, a pretzel factory, etc.

The Wolfawitzes ended up seeing more than they planned. Lots of unexpected things popped up along the route.

When they came back from the vacation, they felt really good. It was easily the best vacation of their lives, and they wondered why.

My father says it was because the Wolfawitzes stopped trying to accomplish anything. They just put a carrot in front of them and decided the carrot wasn't that important but chasing it was.

The story of the Wolfawitzes' vacation was told hundreds of times to hundreds of customers in the small restaurant that my mom and dad ran in Greenwich Village. Each time it was told, my dad would conclude that the vacation changed the Wolfawitzes' whole life, and this was how they were going to live from now on—chasing a very, very small carrot.

The relation that the name Wolfawitz has to Wolfpoint is about the same as Greenwich, England, has to Greenwich Village.

The "Greenwich" of Greenwich Village came from a Dutch village on Long Island called Greenwijck (aka Pine District).

A man named Yellis Mandeville lived on Long Island near Greenwijck. In 1670, Yellis moved to Manhattan, bought a plot of land, and gave it a familiar name.

Copying your old neighbor is an unimaginative way to name a place. I feel this, but I also come from a family that nicknamed their family store "The Store."

The "Village" part came from the fact that in 1670, New York hadn't spread past the lowest tip of Manhattan. Above what is now the seaport and stock exchange were farms, meadows, swamps, woods, and a stream full of trout.

Me or my twin sister on The Store's stoop

The stream full of trout was called Minetta Brook. It was actually called a lot of things, but Minetta is what stuck. The stream wound across downtown Manhattan from what became Gramercy through the future Washington Square Park and dumped out in the Hudson.

Beginning in the 1640s, some freed slaves of the Dutch settled along the Minetta and set up farms and homes.

When yellow fever swept through the crowded tip of Manhattan, people escaped to the village of Greenwijck and the clean waters of the Minetta.

Most of this factual history comes from *The Village*, by John Strausbaugh.

My father says Indians settled Manhattan thanks to antibodies that were found in the Minetta, and that the river is the true source of life where we know it.

This was not mentioned by Strausbaugh. No one calls it the river of life besides my dad.

Well, I call it the river of life, but only in my head.

I am pretty sure my brothers and sisters believe it as well.

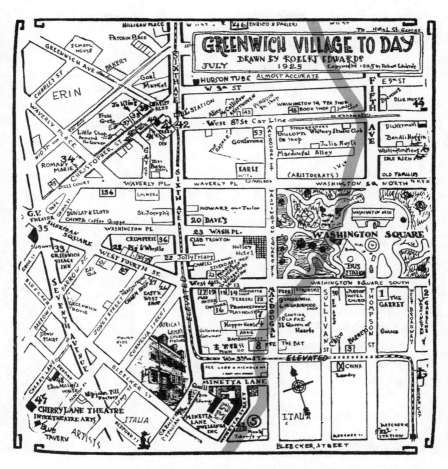

= Minetta Brook's original course

Eventually, as Greenwijck became Greenwich and New York grew, the Village became part of the city. A city that paved over Minetta Brook in 1820. Some streets were shaped and named by it.

The street called Minetta Lane became a subdistrict of the Village known as Little Africa and continued to be settled by freed slaves, now from American owners rather than Dutch. The district had a progressive school and churches, though it was full of poverty, murder, and diseases.

Little Africa was also home to bars known as black-and-tans. Black-and-tans were one of the only spots in the city where white and black people mixed. They were debauched places, with drugs and gambling. Interracial coupling was on the PG side of the place, but they were a heaven for a certain type of person.

As the Village grew, its early acceptance of all people and pro-clivities continued. Blacks could screw whites, whites could screw blacks, men could screw men, musicians could play whatever noise they liked. Things the rest of the country found odd or dis-graceful were welcomed with open arms in the Village. It became a symphony of oddities, and acted as a magnet for the country's fringe people.

But that wasn't what drew my dad.

He answered an ad from a Jewish newspaper that he found in the bathroom of his father's paper factory.

My dad went to see the apartment, which happened to be on Christopher Street.

He loved it.

And was about to sign on the dotted line when he realized how much money it cost.

There was a signing fee, furniture charge every month, rent, and a "rug tax."

He backed out.

Mr. Laverne was not happy. As my dad was leaving, he saw a sign in the building next door.

"Room for rent."

It was a shithole.

But the place was a straight rental with no signing fee or rug tax. And that is how my dad moved to the Village.

WIDE WORLD

My family still owns a restaurant and we still call it "The Store," but it is not "The Store" in my heart.

The one in my heart has a Dutch door and a tiled stoop, surrounded by the sound of roll-down gates with locks and pegs being thrown in a bucket. I am small and dirty with hair my mom calls "the rat's nest."

My twin sister, Minda, has an identical "nest." We step barefoot on tables and take naps in vinyl booths. Charlie, Danny, and Zack, my three brothers, spin on stools and crawl on the floor. Two ceiling fans whirl above covered in dust clumps held together by grease.

And Willoughby stands by the door. He looks cool, even with roast beef hanging from his mouth.

The Store is on the corner of Morton and Bedford Streets in Greenwich Village. And it is still a village.

Everyone knows who we are. Teachers let us say "shit" in class and show up an hour late. "It's not Zack's fault," the real teacher advises the substitute teacher. "He is a Shopsin."

We drag cups across the plastic levers of our family soda fountain and make murder cocktails that contain every flavor.

Customers bring our parents candy and toys from all over the world. The customers are matter-of-fact the best people in New York. New York is matter-of-fact the best place on earth.

Barely 8, my brother Charlie had the day off from school. He told my mom that he wanted to go to the Museum of Natural History. She gave him ten dollars and explained how to take the train to 81st Street.

Charlie crossed the avenue and made his way to the subway.

At the West 4th Street station he paid his token and went to the uptown platform.

But he caught the A train and it didn't stop at 81st.

It didn't stop at 86th or 96th or 103rd.

Charlie got off the train and found a payphone on the platform. It cost a dime.

"Hey, Mom, I'm in Harlem. I'm on 125th Street," Charlie said.

My mom didn't freak out. She told him to go to the downtown side and catch the local C train.

And that is what Charlie did.

At the museum he saw dinosaurs, ran the ramps of the carpeted gem room, ate lunch at the cafeteria, and bought a ruler in the gift shop.

And then he took the train home.

Home was The Store. My mom was not waiting on a nervous edge for Charlie. She was waiting on tables.

When me and my twin sister were older, maybe 11, we would cover shifts for my mom; say, if she needed to go for a parent-teacher meeting. This was always because she had five kids.

Minda was much better at waitressing than me, but we got to split the tips evenly. The tips were huge. We had passbook checking accounts and credit cards.

Whenever my mom was pregnant she'd rub her belly and sing that The Store was about to get a new dishwasher.

On TV I saw kids complain to their parents about doing the dishes and I'd think: fuck, they're only washing one cover, two at most. My brother Danny never complained and he worked whole shifts, whole summers.

He never complained even though I cleared tables like a thoughtless prick, throwing half-full glasses in the bus tray, filling it with a mix of soda and beer.

He did spray me.

None of us thought of working at The Store as a chore.

My dad was the cook. Customers came to talk to him and my mom as much as to eat. It was a forum of philosophy and hot sauce.

Then there was Willoughby, Willy, whose mystery is the reason for this book.

On Mother's Day Willy would poke his head in The Store's double door, a hanger wrapped around his neck. This was his way of celebrating the holiday.

Tic-tac-toe was a quarter a game. Me and Minda were allowed to go into my mom's tip cup for it. Sometimes Willy would let me win, but usually we tied. We played it every day until he taught me craps.

Willy taught my father to curse. If you ever met my dad you know what an achievement that is.

My dad

Albert was a communist, a sailor, and a superintendent. He and my dad were friends and would hang out at a diner on Sheridan Square called Riker's. They'd do the crossword puzzle and eat pastries. This was before The Store and before my mom.

My dad was lost.

Albert suggested he become a super because you didn't have to do much and you got free rent.

So my dad became the live-in super of 38 Morton Street.

In New York at the time, if you had more than five units in a building you needed a live-in super. There was a loophole. You could hire a super that lived within five hundred feet of the building, known as a traveling super. So my dad picked up two more buildings—one on Seventh Avenue and another on Morton Street.

Willy hung around Riker's, too, but at that point, Dad didn't really know him.

It was hard to really know Willy.

He was black, but his skin was silver-white. As a graphic designer now, I can see it as a 10% tint of black. He had a deep voice made for singing without a microphone, and always wore a newsboy cap. He was a senior citizen by the time I was born.

When my oldest brother, Charlie, was little, Willy dubbed him "The Reverend Chuckie Joe" and tried forever to turn him into a boy televangelist.

"But, Willy, I'm Jewish," Charlie would say.

That's better, you a sinner but you seen the light, Willy would reply.

The weekly deposits for The Store were made by Willy. He'd set off with a wad of twenties wrapped in a rubber band and a deposit slip. If there were more twenties than the amount on the slip, Willy got to keep the money.

My mom and dad would mess up now and then. Willy would come back from the bank singing and buy me and my twin sister scratch-off Lotto tickets to celebrate.

My parents put the extra twenties in on purpose.

Mom had no problems with us seeing movies rated PG-13, R, even NC-17. But the skinny dude who worked at the Waverly Theater gave not a shit about what Mom thought, rule is a rule: an adult must accompany you if a movie has a rating above PG. All the movies my brothers wanted to see were above PG.

Willy would take them to see whatever film they wanted. It didn't feel like he was doing them a favor. It felt like a friend, even if they were seeing *Airborne*, a movie whose action sequences involved teenagers rollerblading through Cincinnati.

When it snowed, me and my siblings helped shovel and salt the sidewalk. Not just The Store's sidewalk, but also the sidewalks of the buildings that Willy took care of.

It was Morton Street. That was how my dad and Willy got close. They were both live-in supers.

Very early in my dad's relationship with Willy, they were walking down Morton Street. A man stopped them. "Do you know Willoughby?" the man asked.

Nope, never heard of him, Willy answered.

Time spent with Willy was a lesson. My dad doesn't really know who made the first move in their friendship, but it is safe to assume it wasn't Willy.

World Wide Photo was an image bank and photo-assignment agency. In the 1960s, Willy was looking them up in the phone book. He swapped the name by mistake, searching for Wide World Photo. There was no listing. So he called up the Yellow Pages, bought Wide World Photo, and put his number and address next to it.

In the background of his life, he fielded calls for Wide World. Image requests would come in, he'd turn around and call World Wide, buying the image at a lower rate. He kept popular images on hand.

Willy was, in a way, an artist. He would rather steal ten cents than earn ten dollars.

I found an old stack of photos of the Pope once when I was dropping lunch off at Willy's apartment. It was strange and kind of scared me, because normally I would find photos of tits and ass. I asked my dad, and that's when he told me about Wide World.

Wide World would get calls for photo assignments, too. Assignments to photograph people like Nelson Rockefeller or Cardinal Spellman. My dad would go as Willy's assistant. They'd make fake press passes and have a good time. Willy was a decent photographer. He kept a darkroom in his apartment and had a friend with a stat camera.

My husband, Jason, is a photographer. Some of our first dates were photo jobs where I tagged along as his assistant.

Ever since, I have thought about the Wide World Photo assignments as my dad and Willoughby going out on first dates.

"Ha'yah, mule," Jason would say as I lugged the Profoto pack and light stands. The equipment weighed fifty pounds.

Often I'd get out of balance and crouch so the floor held the burden. Jason would shift the straps and secretly kiss my neck.

This was on the way to shoot things like an animatronic gorilla, the world's largest algae library, a magic trick distributor, the inside of a wind turbine, and the undefeated cookie champions of the Iowa state fair.

Photograph by Jason

I don't know how long Willy's scam went on, but I know how it ended. An accounting agency sent a check meant for World Wide worth $21,000 to Wide World's address, and Willy cashed it. World Wide found out.

Caught, Willy said he would give the money back and then sell them Wide World's Yellow Pages listing.

World Wide said Willy would give the money AND listing back. So he gave both back, and that was that.

Willy was in more than one way an artist. He used to sing at nightclubs.

I wish I could say more, but my dad never went to see Willy sing. That was a separate life. Their life was Morton Street.

A neighborhood guy named Roscoe gave my dad an old safe. The kind you drop on someone in a silent comedy. We still have this safe. Me and my twin sister's first passports are kept in it.

Roscoe had the safe for fifty years but didn't know the combination.

Willy had a friend that was a safecracker.

The safecracker comes. He sees the safe and right off says the last number of this kind is always 17, then zippy-dippy he opens the safe faster than my dad can open it to this day.

Willy had an assortment of friends like that. People who could get you guns. People who could get you drugs. He liked running with dangerous people but had a theory he lived by:

Don't sit next to people like that. Someone might come to shoot them, miss, and get you instead.

The main perk of being a super is not paying rent.

Willy lived in an illegal apartment in the basement of his building.

It wasn't a free ride. Willy worked. He swept the halls, took care of boilers and rats. He was mechanically gifted, with a full set of tools and a never-ending list of requests.

If there was a plumbing problem Willy knew when it was an easy fix and when it was time to call Garboli's.

Garboli was a drunk mess, and he was expensive. But he was better than Two Time Ralph, who no matter what he fixed would need to come back again. Plus Garboli had a plumber named Chris. A thin, sweet guy, Chris would ride over on his bike as soon as you called. There was another good plumber that worked for Garboli named Philip.

Willy and my dad always hoped to get Chris, but were happy as long as Garboli himself didn't show up.

The basement apartment had its own entrance and was sort of hidden. Willy would let people use it as a tryst spot for secret love affairs.

One morning Willy woke up and found a gun dropped in his window. He took it apart and dumped it in the river.

Memphis was a friend you didn't sit next to. Willy never let him near my dad. If Willy was talking to Memphis my dad circled the block.

Memphis wouldn't drop a gun in Willy's window if he wanted it back.

But one of Memphis's lackeys would. When the kid came looking for the gun Willy chewed him out.

Fucking shit. You don't dump no gun in my house without telling me.

When Willy told this story to my father it was long, lyrical, and involved two women. Nuances like that are now lost to time.

Willy never had to pay for drinks; he would just sing a set at a club or be treated by someone. And he didn't pay for other things, because people owed him for the use of his love nest. He learned to survive in the city like an Indian lives off the land.

"The nutrients of New York City are in the fringe people." I was brought up to believe this, and that the definition of a fringe person was Willoughby.

Willy was born in St. Louis. His mother had tried to abort him and ran off as soon as she could. He was raised by his dad, who worked for the railroad.

As a kid Willy got a lot of shit for being light-skinned. An ungodly amount. I think his dad was black and his mom was a mix. There must have been some Irish, because he had red hair. I can't confirm this, because I only knew him with gray tiny curls. But he would tell me about getting the crap kicked out of him. He must have looked pretty freaky, because as a person Willy was the least contentious human on the planet.

A blind woman named Annie lived in Willy's building. Annie baked these fluffy muffins. She always gave a few to Willy because he helped her out and because he loved them.

One day Willy is over at her apartment. She is baking the muffins and measures out the ingredients. There are hundreds of bugs and weevils crawling in not just the flour but the sugar, too.

He never told Annie about the bugs. He just continued to eat the muffins. And he loved the muffins just the same.

But when pushed, Willy would get tough. His father had taught him to fight back.

Willy didn't know where to begin.

There were so many kids that beat him up.

Start with the biggest, scariest one, was his father's advice.

A boy named Arvell was twice anyone's size. One day Willy walks by Arvell and baits him into a fight. As soon as Arvell swings, Willy hits him in the shin with a copper pipe.

Willy didn't win the pipe fight. But he won the war: no one bothered him after that. For the rest of his life he didn't take crap from anyone.

He taught it to my dad, and he taught it to me:

Stand up to that cocksucking bully. No shit if you lose. As long as it ain't a free ride, that motherfucker, all those motherfuckers, will let you be.

Later Arvell and Willy became friends, and that made double sure no one messed with him.

When he moved to New York, Willy brought a wife. She was beautiful, but a compulsive gambler who would fuck other guys, and eventually did too much coke. I never met her. I never met any of Willy's ladies. Separate life.

Willoughby loved pussy. There is nothing more in this wide world he loved more than pussy. It is just a fact.

My dad told me Willy once had a girl over. The girl and Willy had lots of sex and drinks. And he gave her his television set.

When Willy wanted to get laid he gave everything away. He had an expression:

When I'm hard I'm soft and when I'm soft I'm hard.

And it was true, because the next day Willy went and got the television back.

WOLF'S LAIR

Parking costs ten zloty. We are in the middle of nowhere.

When I was 11 my whole family drove to Dollywood, Dolly Parton's theme park in Pigeon Forge, Tennessee.

We sang "Dolly Parton is the best. She's got mountains on her chest" the whole way there.

It was far.

Finally a roller coaster peeked out from hickory trees. "We're glad you're here!" a sign proclaimed.

"Parking $10," said another.

My dad turned the car around. Five children banged on the glass wailing and begging. My mom hummed "9 to 5" as we drove away forever.

Jason downshifts the rental car. I remember that ten zloty is less than four dollars and let it go.

A checkpoint has three guards smoking cigarettes. They don't have any official badge or uniform, unless well-defined muscles count as a uniform.

The biggest one comes over to our car.

Jason hesitates before he rolls down the window.

Forty zloty later, we are past the razor wire fence.

I am relieved to find three giant tour buses in the parking lot, signaling we are not the only humans here.

Here is the eastern edge of Poland, at what remains of Hitler's headquarters called Wolf's Lair.

Surrounded by swamps, lakes, and woods, the location was picked for its remoteness but also for its proximity to the Soviet Union, which Hitler wanted to invade.

Our reasons for visiting Wolf's Lair are less clear.

Last night I said to Jason: "There is an old Nazi bunker three hours away. I'm creeped out by it, but do you want to go see it?"

"Definitely," he replied.

Wood-and-concrete bunkers were built. Wolf's Lair became a small city with two air strips, a casino, its own power generator, a railway station, and a cinema.

This info is learned from a guide I downloaded to my phone. Keeping in the spirit of a Nazi bunker more than a historic site, Wolf's Lair doesn't provide much information or guidance. Except a big wooden map similar to the kind that ski resorts have. Rather than K2 trails and bunny slopes, it marks the bunkers of Hitler and Göring.

Past the ski map are a hotel and a café housed in an original bunker that wasn't destroyed.

Bare bones and army green, the sparseness of the café looks almost hip. The coffee is not bad.

A sign that resembles a beat-up dog tag reads "Souvenirs." The small kiosk sells snacks and World War II novelties. I buy a history map pamphlet with 𝔚𝔬𝔩𝔣'𝔰 𝔏𝔞𝔦𝔯 set in Jackboot Grotesk. Jason buys some crackers.

Hitler spent over eight hundred days at Wolf's Lair. In the early mornings he would receive frontline reports, from nine to ten he would take his dog for a walk, and at night he would drift off serenaded by the ribbit, ribbit of frogs.

The lair had a mosquito problem due to all the nearby swamps. It wasn't just a problem, it was a plague. Some of the guards wore beekeeper hats to protect themselves.

To fix the plague the soldiers poured oil in all the swamps. This killed off the mosquitoes, but it also killed all the frogs.

Hitler was pissed.

A batch of frogs had to be imported ASAP.

We follow a German tour group into the woods. Their guide speaks into a portable PA that he carries like a purse. Jason and I don't understand German, so it sounds like another tacky decorating decision the lair made.

The mosquitoes are gigantic. I slather bug spray on Jason and myself.

Wolf's Lair was protected on the ground by land mines and barbed wire fences; it was hidden by air through camouflage nets and strategic overgrowth.

Witnessing the strength of the Soviets, Hitler didn't think the lair was safe enough. Bunkers were reenforced. More land mines were added.

In November 1944, things started to go downhill, and Hitler ordered the destruction of Wolf's Lair. Eighteen thousand pounds of dynamite was no match for the lair. Most of the buildings were damaged, but not many destroyed. The soldiers gave up, and the ruins of Wolf's Lair still stand today.

They are remarkably intact. Each bunker is numbered, and you can enter. There are bits of rebar and chunks of concrete sprinkled throughout. The forest is overgrown, and the path is more of a hiking trail.

Yellow signs, spray-painted on rubble and rocks, warn that the bunkers are old and liable to fall, you shouldn't stray from the trail, as there might still be undiscovered land mines, and under no circumstance should you climb the bunkers.

Everyone is climbing the bunkers, especially a group of Polish teenagers and Jason.

Claus von Stauffenberg tried to assassinate Hitler at Wolf's Lair. Von Stauffenberg came very close to success. So close there was a Tom Cruise movie made about the attempt.

The bunker where the attempt took place has a monument to von Stauffenberg, and the longest blurb in my walking tour guide.

Moss-covered traces of the war are at every turn. It is not just moving, but haunting. Jason and I both imagine hearing gunfire.

Wolf's Lair is off. I am surprised that it has not been boycotted. It seems only a matter of time before an angry mob will demand the lair cease operating a military-themed hotel and canteen. It will be deemed poor taste and a celebration of a monster. This faction will also demand the guards of Wolf's Lair not be so threatening and not quite so ripped. Crushing cans with your shoulder blades will not be part of the employment test. Guards won't be allowed or encouraged to wear black army boots. And they will be called guides, not guards.

But right now, amid the tactlessness, insensitivity, and genuine confusion of how to present such a place, Wolf's Lair spurs more thoughts and emotions than a respectful plaque with fact-checked details could.

It wasn't our imagination.

Inside bunker number seventeen we find a guy in camo pants, renting replica World War II rifles for a few zloty.

It is a shooting range. The targets are glass bottles hung on strings.

Two women wearing matching visors poke their heads in, make grossed-out faces, and hightail it to the next bunker. Camo pants seems used to this.

A SEVEN-DAY PILLBOX

Before he dropped out of college my dad did a report on *The Catcher in the Rye*. He focused on the part of the plot where Holden keeps wondering where the ducks go when the pond freezes. Holden wonders, does a guy come in a truck and take them or do they just fly away? My dad went to Central Park and asked.

The ducks just stay there and take care of themselves.

What I took from this story was not so much the ducks being able to take care of themselves but my dad asking for help from Central Park.

When I was in college, Willy was seventy-something with a cane.

He still came to The Store every day. My dad screwed a huge silver handle next to the door so Willy could manage the stoop himself.

Willy would sit in his favorite booth, and I would bring him a sweet potato and a birch beer. Often I would help him home because he lived on the second floor.

One day he came in and told my dad he was going to Germany for a singing gig.

The next day he came in and said he had a great time and now had a show in Paris.

Then Willoughby didn't come in.

We had keys to his place. I went and all his stuff was there, but I didn't see Willy.

I'm a little foggy, and what I write may unintentionally lack the whole truth. Names changed, facts left out, facts put in. Memory is unreliable, especially with an event that can't be seen from the other side.

This I know: Willy must have been with two thousand girls just on Morton Street. Married women, young, old, white, black, long-term, short-term, crazy, sane. They all loved Willy, and when I say loved I mean fucked. He only was really married to Yvonne, and she was a bitch that broke his heart and she was dead. He had no children. He hated his family, and his mother, father were definitely dead.

Willy and my father had been together for decades. He was our blood. There was always an understanding my dad would take care of Willy, but I don't think any of us imagined there would be a day when Willy couldn't take care of himself.

At this point I was 19 and lived by myself in an apartment above The Store. I was sort of the super of my building. I swept the halls, took care of the trash, changed fuses, but I paid rent because I had a rent-stabilized apartment.

In NYC some apartments have regulated rents that keep them affordable and give the tenant rights that make it hard to be kicked out. Willoughby had swapped his illegal basement apartment for a rent-stabilized apartment as well.

Basically, an R.S. apartment is a golden ticket that allows you to live in a city you love but could not afford otherwise. It is not fair, but neither is life.

The best stoop on Morton Street was Willy's building. It was wide, so you didn't need to stand up as people entered or exited. Before he had The Store, my father would sit on that stoop and shoot the breeze with Willy all day. The building used to be owned by Judge Massey, who lived on Park Avenue.

On the second floor lived Don, a singer, with his wife, who was a great pianist. Willy used to sing duets with her. One day she wasn't feeling well. The one day turned into twenty. So she went to St. Vincent's, they told her she had a virus and should go home and just rest.

That night her appendix ruptured and she died.

Don survived the eviction trial because they were married.

On the third floor lived the Strauks. Arnold and Margaret had two or three boys. Arnold made his living cleaning Jewish temples. Margaret was Scottish and baked great shortbread cookies. Before The Store became a restaurant it was a neighborhood grocery, and my dad would sell Margaret's cookies.

The Store sold baked goods from lots of people over the years. All of them lived within a few blocks. Lester worked for the board of education and baked linzer tortes on the side. Crystal was a hippie and it was her main source of income, but she never made the same kind of cookies twice. And Kathleen baked the best chocolate chip cookies ever made.

Kathleen fell deeply in love with baking chocolate chip cookies. She took care in the tiniest details, like how you crumble the brown sugar. If the weather was humid she would crumble less.

People were hooked on Kathleen's cookies and would stop into The Store throughout the day looking for them. The cookies were how Robert De Niro beefed up for *Raging Bull*.

Because of the way the cookies were made she could only bake twelve at a time. So she had them baking in the background all day. She lived three doors down and would bring them over in her bare feet.

Kathleen never wore shoes. She ran a school from her house, had three kids who broke all the IQ tests, was a full-time professor and accomplished author, but to us she was "the cookie lady."

Margaret Strauk made a lot of money on the cookies my dad sold, but the Strauks never bought anything in our store. The Store really wasn't expensive. We sold cans of tuna fish and jars of jam. The fanciest thing was melon ball salad. But the Strauks were the cheapest people on the planet.

All the bathrooms in Willy's building were in the hall. Not a strange thing at the time. The toilet seat in the third-floor bathroom was so old that the enamel had worn off. Arnold wouldn't buy a new seat because he thought it was the judge's responsibility.

One day my dad and Willy are on the stoop. Arnold starts hounding Willy about the toilet seat. Willy finally just says something like:

The judge has got a penthouse and a servant. How you going to fuck him up by getting splinters in your ass? He ain't going to give you no toilet seat. He wish you would all fuckin' leave, an' he get more rent; he is one greedy cocksucker!

I don't know if Arnold took the hint and bought one, but he didn't bug Willy about the seat anymore.

Years later my dad hired Arnold's son Brian to be a delivery boy. An order came in and Brian was sent with it.

But Brian came back with the order. He couldn't find Clarkson Street. My dad explained to him it was a block away from Leroy Street, but he still didn't understand where it was. Finally my dad mentioned it was near the park with the pool, and Brian understood.

Brian was 15 years old and didn't know any street names.

My dad didn't interpret this as Brian being stupid; he understood that Morton Street and the blocks it touched were more than enough for anyone's existence.

Actually, Willy was married four times.

Yvonne was the first and the only real one. They were wed in St. Louis. She was awful. Cheated on Willy with Joe Louis. Gambled or snorted away his money.

Next came Pilar. Who Willy described like so:

She offered me three thousand dollars. Sure, what the fuck. I'll marry ya. I'll have your kid for another five hundred.

And then he did two more citizenship marriages, one in New Jersey and another in Pennsylvania.

The courts weren't very on top of it at that point, or Willy knew who to grease. He never got divorced once.

Immigration didn't come after him, but he was ready if they wanted to interview him. He had slept with all his fake wives. Not as part of the sham; they didn't need to. Willy just charmed them into it.

There was a yellow bank check for $80,000 with dot matrix printed numbers and my father's name. Willy had given it to my father a month earlier with some kind of instructions. I don't know what they were, but the gist of it was, don't cash it until I tell you to or I die. Looking back, this should have been a huge red flag, but my dad was running a restaurant, had five kids, and Willoughby was always up to something.

Standing in Willy's apartment, I was scared. Maybe he fell down somewhere. Could he be in Paris? The place was a mess, but it was always a mess. His dresser drawers were half full, but I'd never looked in his dresser drawers. There was a box of condoms and a photo of Yvonne. How could Willy go to Paris when he rarely crossed Seventh Avenue?

I walked the half a block to The Store. "He's not there," I said, shaking my head.

My dad told the waitress (my mom) to hold the checks, finished the soup he was cooking, and left the kitchen.

Wearing his apron and sweatband, a pencil tucked behind his ear, my dad walked up and down Morton Street.

Here it falls apart in my head. I think my father found Willy after walking up and down the block upset.

He found him in the same crummy basement apartment Willy had lived in decades ago. The apartment with the window that guns were dropped in and where everyone took their secret lovers.

Willy told my dad that the new building owner had moved him down there because there were less stairs. Then he said to deposit the check because he didn't want the doctors to get it. Which was maybe illegal. Which makes this story true to me, because Willy was always on a scam.

But I don't really know. All the events surrounding Willy are foggy.

I know my dad was pissed that Willy had let himself be moved down there. My dad had worked hard to make sure Willy had an R.S. apartment with a lease.

I visited Willy in the basement and brought him a bowl of chili. He called me sugar pie and asked why I didn't bring a birch beer. No talk of Paris, though he did mention Josephine Baker's tits.

But the next day he was on another planet. I left through the narrow hall, up the steps beneath the best stoop on Morton Street, and thought that I'd come back later and he would be Willy. And that is what happened, but I knew he was now liable to disappear at any moment.

The check didn't go through. Someone had frozen the account.

That someone was the landlord. The Garrisons had recently bought Willy's building. It was a trio of sisters who owned a bunch of other buildings.

In the midst of this I was commuting to college upstate, learning about things like Herbert Bayer's Universal Alphabet—a typeface that had mixed lower- and uppercase letters in an attempt to make typography more efficient. In my downtime I read thick books about vaudeville.

fatty
buster
little tramp
gracie
schnozzola

Herbert Bayer's 1925 Universal Alphabet in use

This was before cell phones. Maybe some people had them, but no one in my family.

Somehow we found out that it was specifically Denise Garrison who had moved Willy to the basement and now had power of attorney.

I was visiting Willy two times a day with food, newspapers, and porno magazines wrapped in brown paper. My dad was fat and could hardly fit in the hall that led to Willy's apartment. Even if he was thin I don't think he would have visited more.

My dad got a lawyer who said he needed to take power of attorney back. So my dad squeezed down there with the lawyer, and Willy signed power of attorney over to my dad. No problem.

And the next thing we knew, Willy was in the Village nursing home. And Denise Garrison had power of attorney again.

My mom was just a peanut in all this. She wasn't close with Willy. They had never been mean to each other, and they had no harsh thoughts of the other, but there was no relationship between them.

The kindest soul. No one kinder on the planet. That is what fills my brain when I think of my mom. I should give an example of why this is so, but my mind goes blank. We were not that close, and we will never be.

She died in a blink when I was barely twenty-three.

My sister, Minda, was my mom. She was the one I told when I got my period. I told Minda and Minda told Mom. That was the way it worked.

I got my dad to visit Willy at the nursing home.

Just to visit.

And we shot the shit and that would have been it.

But as we were leaving, a curtain in Willy's room opened to reveal an old woman sleeping with a single rose in a vase. The curtain was opened by a thin guy who introduced himself as Hazel. He told us a woman was here signing my grandpa up for Medicaid and a cemetery plot yesterday. Then he added that the woman was up to no good. Hazel asked to exchange phone numbers so he could tell us if the woman named Denise came back.

This changed things.

It might not add up in a neat package but these are the things I remember.

Willy was getting healthier. I signed him out for a walk. We sat in the park and he told me about this shithead friend he had as a kid who would use snakes as lassos and snap their heads off.

From the bench I saw a bank.

My relationship with Willy was not one where I could talk about what I wanted. We never talked about Bayer's Universal Alphabet or Harpo Marx. And I couldn't bring up the registered check he gave my dad or power of attorney.

It felt a little illicit. But this was the way Willy liked things to feel.

I asked Willy if he wanted to go to the bank tomorrow and he said he did.

A few days later, me and my sister signed Willy out and met my dad at the bank across from the home. I am not sure how my dad still had the check Willy gave us like it was brand-new, but he did. And the four of us sat with an agent and talked about opening an account.

The agent was female with a low-cut blouse and Willy hit on her the whole time. If she had asked for the $80,000 he would have given it to her.

I am not sure what we were doing at the bank. Whatever it was didn't take. All I know is, Willy left with a hard-on and had peed all over the bank's chair.

My sister's memory of this day is even more foggy than mine, but she remembers the pee as well.

My dad hired another lawyer. This one wrote a threatening letter to the Garrisons. It accused them of taking advantage of an old man, moving him out of his R.S. apartment, and stealing his money. It alluded to the fact that the grace which they performed this act was too great for it to have been the first time. It said Willy didn't need to be in a nursing home and that he better have an apartment to live in when he got back.

In the mail my father received a $60,000 check from Denise Garrison's personal account, and the paperwork for the cemetery plot she had signed Willy up for.

Willoughby was released and moved back into the basement, to which I was given a set of keys.

Morton Street went back to normal, except I now picked up Willy's prescriptions, and once a week would split the medicine into a seven-day pillbox.

And every night I brought him dinner.

Sweet potatoes, chili, fresh turkey, tuna salad, steamed broccoli, whole wheat toast, egg salad on rye, sloppy joe, BLT, pea soup, brisket, pulled pork, roast beef, potato chips, and pecan pie. Always with a birch beer.

There were other dishes, but these were his favorites. It all came from The Store.

The pie was baked by me. I baked two a week, my mom paid me eight dollars a pie. She sold it for $2.25 a slice with fresh whipped cream. It was a good deal for me because I didn't pay for the ingredients.

Willy would sit at the table in the small shitty basement apartment with half a window and none of his stuff. He would eat his sloppy joe, happy as fuck. And it was like the whole episode never happened. He didn't ask about Denise or his things.

So I never asked either.

And maybe the fact that we didn't talk about it all was proof that Willy still had some badass in him.

I regret not asking where his photos went.

I had to buy a pillbox with bigger compartments.

Willy's hands started to shake. We bought him an electric razor.

He couldn't make it down the block on his own anymore. His cane was replaced with a walker. I got him a phone with giant buttons to call us if he wanted to leave the basement, and taped this note to his wall:

KENNY & MARA
924-5160 / 414-9674

I commuted to class three days a week. My twin sister, Minda, went to the same school, SUNY Purchase, but she lived up there like a normal student.

My twin sister had the first cell phone of us all. I wasn't allowed to call it. She did a study abroad year in London, and the phone was only for an emergency. There was a landline in her dorm I could call with a calling card. I'd spend ten minutes dialing and then if I was lucky enough to reach her, we'd speak till the card ran out. This was hours, not minutes. It was the farthest I had ever been from her and it hurt.

Recently the Dollywood road trip came up. My sister remembered it differently than me.

In her version my dad pulled up to the gate and let Mom out of the car to check the ticket price for two adults and five kids.

Three hundred dollars was the cost. My parents debated this figure, while we kids held our breath.

It was decided the three hundred dollars was a good investment. We all cheered.

We are going to Dollywood!

Then came the parking lot in the middle of nowhere that cost ten dollars, the car full of crying kids, my mom humming "9 to 5" as we drove away forever.

Minda also recalls that after we had stopped crying and humming "9 to 5," we passed a firework store.

"That is where we got the pagoda," my sister said.

Me (left) and Minda in Washington Square Park

And just like that I realized her version was righter than mine; memories flooded in.

My dad made a U-turn. He and my mom didn't even need to discuss it. It was just a fact. The earth rotates around the sun; the Shopsin family needed to buy three hundred dollars' worth of fireworks.

Seven baskets were filled with blackjacks, roman candles, silver fountains, paper tanks, and more than a child can imagine. Then bottle rockets were added on top to round us up to exactly three hundred dollars.

That night we set them all off.

An octagon-shaped firework was lit. It spun, spitting out sparks in a coil. When the smoke cleared it had popped up into a five-story structure.

The firework was called the "Friendship Pagoda." Me and Minda had picked it out together. It was the undisputed winner of the night.

I gave all the time I didn't spend with my sister to Willy.

Willy spoke to me differently than he spoke to other people. It always had a sweet kiddo vibe to it, even if he was talking about Madonna's thighs.

There was this big truck
Filled with apples
All that stood between me
An them apples was a gate

So I just loosened the gate
A little

Gently

G e n t l y

G e n t l y

So all the fucking apples come out
Spill out all over

But nobody seen me
So I hides behind a tree
Just when I hear a man comin

"God damn!
Look at
That
Can't have anything"

So I go out like I just
Come upon him
An help him pick up them big
Red apples

An then to pay me back
for picking up the apples
he gives me a dollar an some apples

Willy you're bad

Huh
But I picked em all up

But he gave you a dollar

Yeah
An the apples was so big
An yummy, too
Almost good as this time I decided to steal some watermelons

Willy

So I put em in my little wagon
But they was too heavy

I couldn't pull it
So I only took threee

When I got home my aunt asked
Where'd I get those watermelons
I said, "The guy down the street there
Well well why he gave em to me"
I told a big lie you know

So I took em in the backyard
I had a big butcher knife
An I sliced em

Oh god
Oh god
They was good
They was good

Good

The juice red

An such a beautiful color red
Oh man I ate em with seeds an everything
Ahhh god all of it running an sweet

And my aunt asked again

Don't you know those days always somebody gave me something

    Willy you're bad

Well
Shit

I had to live somehow my father never gave me nothing

I was always in trouble
You know
Always always always
But one time

One time

I went to church
And the preacher was preaching
Preaching preaching preaching preaching a sermon
He was talking about going to hell an all these things
I got real scared

An then I told a friend of mine
He scared me bad
An my friend said I don't think he'll do anything to you
You didn't know any better

Oh yeah I says
That's right

I didn't know any better
I didn't know any better

The sweet kiddo vibe was double thick in the basement. He talked about his friend Mickey a lot. We'd play blackjack for nickels, but he'd get tired fast. Willy was losing weight. His limbs had become rigid like a paper skeleton with grommets for elbows.

Sometimes before I left he'd grab my hand and wouldn't say anything. He would squeeze softly, and we would smile at each other.

I never squeezed back. I was afraid I would crush his fingers.

Now and again a story would go super blue, the kiddo voice would disappear, and a truckload of curses would be unleashed.

When this happened Willy felt like my grandpa.

Not my real grandpa, who wore a hat with a ferret painted on it. My dad's dad, who seemed to hate us foul-mouthed dirtballs.

Willy liked it when I cursed. It was easy to make him smile. All I had to do was call something or someone "motherfucker." And every time I said "motherfucker" I would wonder if my dad had come from Willy instead of the ferret.

We got Willy a part-time nurse named Sonia. Willy loved her; well, he loved that she had breasts and was fair game.

I was off-limits, not because I was young, but because I was Kenny's kid and for all intents and purposes Willy's granddaughter. It also helped that I looked and dressed like a 12-year-old boy.

I wish I could remember one of the thousand lines he used on Sonia. More often than not it was funny and harmless, with Willy winking as he said it. Sometimes it worked and Sonia would flirt back. But other times it was relentless and creepy. When she'd help him bathe he would be hard as a rock, smiling. So she quit. I didn't blame her.

I didn't blame Gladys either. Or Anya or Mary. I would have quit, too. Finally the service had to stop sending women.

And if I had realized what it meant, I wouldn't have gone along with it, but it didn't occur to me that pussy was what was keeping Willy present.

The thing I hated most was the pillbox. I was afraid I would mess up. There were so many pills, and each had specific instructions.

That's not true. Dementia was what I hated most.

One day Willy hit on me as I was changing his diaper. He asked why we couldn't have a quick fuck.

The nurse that lasted the longest was named Cardinal. He was from the West Indies, short with a thick accent. He had a beautiful Spenserian script handwriting that was sometimes impossible to understand.

Shopping:

Wetwipes

Paper towels

Boraxo

Q-tips

Palmolive

Cardinal was always reading the Bible. He only talked about Jesus, salvation, and keeping the bathroom clean. Willy hated him.

I would try to bring other videos, but there were just three Willy ever wanted to see: *The Snows of Kilimanjaro*, *The Josephine Baker Story*, and a bootleg cam video of *Notting Hill*, starring Julia Roberts and Hugh Grant.

When I'd start to play a new video, he would say, You ever see that one with Julia Roberts?

Yeah, Willy, I have a copy of it here.

Then what we watching this shit for?

In 1983, the Bottle Bill (aka, the Returnable Container Law) was enacted.

Under the law, if you bought a bottled or canned beverage you paid a five-cent deposit. Any business that sold bottled or canned beverages had to be ready to give anyone five cents back in exchange for the bottle or can. The same hokeypokey was then performed between the business and the city.

The law was meant to encourage recycling. And it did.

With homeless people.

My dad wanted nothing to do with the law. He didn't want the empty sticky bottles attracting roaches and he didn't want to deal with the lines of homeless people with shopping carts full of cans and bottles.

So he called up Coca-Cola and asked about soda fountain machines.

"I can solve your bottle problem, and make you fifty thousand dollars a year," said the salesman.
"You don't make fifty thousand a year, do ya?" my dad asked.
"No."
"Then why don't you buy a soda machine?"
"Well, you can't sell someone soda unless they are already in your place as a customer. You have a nice line for your deli. People buying sandwiches, gum, chips. A soda machine is what you need."

Sometimes a salesman tells the truth.

The soda machine not only solved the Bottle Bill problem, it freed up refrigerator space. No more restocking said fridge, no chance of it being shoplifted, no sell-by dates because it was made fresh, but most of all it made money. The profit margin on fountain soda is like a superpower.

Miniature garden hoses ran from The Store to the basement below, where the carbonator and tanks of syrup lived. Before I learned to tie my shoes, I knew how to detach and reattach the syrup nozzle of our soda machine.

You could control the taste of the soda by adjusting a screw on the fountain head. The perfect ratio of syrup to soda became my dad's undying passion.

Every time the syrup was changed, we all tasted the soda and compared notes.

The Store was full of these little passions. My parents were happy.

They were running their own place, their way, with customers they loved.

Then the landlord raised the rent, big-time.

The Store as it was couldn't make that amount of money ever, not on cat food and Cheerios.

So my parents decided to turn The Store into a restaurant. Not because they didn't love running a grocery store or had some long-harbored chef fantasy.

They changed The Store to a restaurant because my dad thought it would sell more soda.

The restaurant thing worked; we sold lots of soda and paid lots of rent.

And The Store was still special and full of little passions. We still called it The Store even though it was a restaurant.

On Saturdays I helped my dad shop. We'd supplement The Store's wholesale orders with a produce market on Hamilton Avenue, a supermarket in New Jersey, and a cash-and-carry where we mostly bought candy.

After anybody ate at The Store they were allowed to take free candy from a huge display that ran down a pink marble counter. Candy of every type: Tootsie Rolls, Junior Mints, Smarties, gummies, peanut butter cups, Hershey's Kisses, Mr. Goodbar, Nerds, and on and on. Once someone said they couldn't eat candy because of their rotten teeth. My dad added a jar of disposable toothbrushes. The kind with the toothpaste inside. When you squeezed the handle the paste would squish through the plastic bristles.

Customers that traveled would bring gifts back for us, maybe as a way to repay the candy debt. Things like:

A glass soda bottle from Asia that had a marble which regulated the flow of soda to make sure you didn't guzzle.

A candy called "ant piss" from Amsterdam that tasted just like sawdust and lemon concentrate.

A soft tan drawstring pouch made from a kangaroo's balls.

An origami shirt made of Japanese yen my mom taped to the fridge.

A floaty pen of Ronald Reagan that when you turned it, his clothes came off.

One of the supermarkets where my dad and I shopped was decorated with plastic grapes. They were placed in every aisle like Easter eggs. All kinds: red, green, Champagne, Concords, Muscats. Some with little green ivy leaves and tendrils, others with brown stems pressed with fake wood grain.

One bunch at a time, the grapes started coming home with me.

I hung them all in the entrance to my bathroom, making the grapes dangle above.

At the time I washed all my clothes in the bathtub. I loved it to an illogical degree.

Channeling photos of old New York with clotheslines strung across every building, I ran one on a hypotenuse from my fire escape to my farthest window.

Washboards had become expensive antiques that decorated bed and breakfasts, so I'd fill the tub, roll my pants up, and stomp and swish as if I was Lucille Ball making wine.

And the grapes set the scene, semitranslucent with the sun shining through.

At the cash-and-carry, I started buying Willy Ensure, a beverage that a doctor had recommended to help him gain weight. It was a complete meal in a can.

For a while it was liquid all day, and I'd bring solid food at night and feed him like you do a baby.

Then he could only eat liquids. So I'd bring a birch beer as a treat.

His deep voice became a whisper. Sometimes he would have me lean in close and he'd tell me Yvonne was at the window trying to get in.

She come to steal my money. That fucking bitch.

Willoughby had an attack and went to the hospital by ambulance. The doctors thought it was only going to get worse and it was best to send him to a home.

I never visited him. I don't think. Maybe once me and my dad went by motorcycle. Maybe it was awful and he didn't know who we were.

I know I never went down to the basement again.

My bathroom entrance grew to include the bathroom ceiling. I strung wire, not string, knowing in a few months the string would snap from the weight.

At bunch No. 70 it got harder to steal the grapes.

This was because No. 70 was the last bunch of grapes in the supermarket, not because security had cracked the case.

No one at the supermarket seemed to notice the grapes had ever existed.

This was good: I never got caught. This was bad: nobody ever came to replace them.

I was sad.

And it gave me pause.

But then I passed a wine shop.

The window had hundreds of plastic grapes.

The collecting continued.

I can't remember when Willy died. My dad got the call and I was shocked, because I thought Willy was dead already.

HOLE 18

The entryway has a rack of tourist pamphlets: rafting, go-karts, and Frank Lloyd Wright's Fallingwater.

Jason comes out of the bathroom. He's surprised I didn't know Fallingwater was in Pennsylvania. A quote on the brochure describes Fallingwater as "a house that summed up the 20th century" and Wright's "most sublime integration of man and nature." Jason calls the ticket office.

There is only one tour opening. It begins in forty minutes. We can make it but would have to leave right now. This makes the decision easy, though I've heard Fallingwater's gift shop has a few gems.

We are standing on top of the largest cave in Pennsylvania, but we've actually come for what is advertised in the putt-putt pamphlet.

KAVERNPUTT

AT

LAUREL CAVERNS

Opened in 1999, Kavernputt was built to be a wheelchair accessible cavern with "the broader purpose" of an eighteen-hole miniature golf course.

I give the cashier a ten, and she gives me two balls and two putters. We go through a wooden saloon door with a snap spring.

It's dark and the walls and ceilings feel like the fake rocks you hide keys in. It is way better than I imagined. There is a little bit of a grandpa's basement smell. But if it weren't for the Astroturf and ADA-compliant pathways, Kavernputt could look like a real cave.

The golf course is difficult, mostly because it is very dark. There are no windmills, only rock formations.

My night vision kicks in and I get a hole in one. Jason gets a hole in six. This can't last.

It doesn't.

All of the holes have a geological theme and employ different tricks. They are charming and inspired. The hole about echoes has voice-activated lights. I repeat "echo" over and over, making them flicker.

In ancient Greece, Zeus was saved by a cave. His mom, Rhea, hid him in one. She did this so Zeus's father, Cronus, wouldn't eat him. Rhea then wrapped a rock in swaddling clothes and gave it to Cronus.

Cronus swallowed the fake baby ASAP, because it was foretold that one of his sons would overpower him.

My father would never have eaten the rock baby.

One of his core beliefs is that as a parent you shouldn't try to be too wonderful. Being perfect makes it so your children can't compare and gives them a complex.

If you set the bar low your kids are sure to at least be more successful than you.

Zeus grew up to overthrow Cronus. He also grew up to swallow his unborn baby and wife.

14

(par 3)

EARTHQUAKE
ROOM

That is all we are telling you about this hole.

I point out a homemade stalagmite that slumps like a soft penis. Jason laughs but still sinks the putt.

We love the course and consider it a work of art, but are both relieved as hole 18 swallows our balls for good.

THINGS

As kids my dad would take us each on walk nights. There were five of us, and rather than try to give us all attention at once, he would split us up. Every night was a different kid.

A walk could be simple as crossing Seventh Avenue to the Mexican restaurant called Caliente Cab Co. Not to eat—they had a giant plastic margarita bolted onto the wall. It hung twenty feet above with a permanent tidal wave of dripping foam. My dad would stand under it, head tilted back and tongue sticking out. He would rub his belly and say how good it tasted. And I would do the same, only more. Squinting my eyes, pulling on his hand as I tilted back, saying it was the best margarita I had ever tasted.

That was my brother Zack's favorite walk. He was forever asking, "Can we go drink the margarita?" We all had our favorite spot.

My brother Danny loved to go to the Chinatown arcade, where he would pay a quarter to lose to, and one time tie, the tic-tac-toe-playing chicken. Minda loved to go to a bar on Seventh Avenue named McBell's and drink a Shirley Temple while my dad drank Diet Coke.

Mine was the Waverly Diner. I'd pick our seats at the counter, and Dad would ask what I wanted as I hopped on the stool.

But he knew what I wanted: a fresh-squeezed orange juice.

Across from us was a fully automated orange juicing machine. The oranges sat in a cage on top. When we would order, the waiter in a black vest would flip a switch. The machine would come to life and 8-year-old me would float above the earth with delight.

Once a man was sitting next to us. He got a hot water with lemon and nursed it. Then he added sugar to his ice water and dropped his used-up lemon wedge in. Dad and I were at the diner a long time and left at the same time as the hot-water guy. His check was twenty-five cents and he left a five-cent tip. Our check was fifteen dollars and my dad left a five-dollar tip.

My dad never really taught us to believe in God. He did teach us: If you like the service, leave a good tip. If you like the restaurant, buy a soda or an iced tea.

I'm sure we both had fountain Diet Cokes along with my fresh OJ. The check was likely filled out by an English muffin, a goblet of red Jell-O cubes, and a cup of chili.

Hot-water guy and us walked south on Sixth Avenue. As we approached St. Joseph's my dad switched places with me so he would be the one next to the vagrants on the steps. There was always a mess of them because St. Joseph's gave away free soup.

We were behind hot-water guy, who we had decided was a mooch and wouldn't ever let him sit in our restaurant making lemonade from our sugar.

Then hot-water guy stopped and talked to the panhandlers. He put a dollar in each of the bums' cups. And my dad's jaw dropped.

We didn't give money to bums. We gave money to small businesses because we knew how hard it was to make rent in New York.

My dad would tell that story a thousand times. Each time drawing a new and deeper meaning, positioning himself as an ignorant asshole, speculating that this might be the root of our problems as a nation, that we don't feel enough sympathy for people who are not like us.

The meat and potatoes of a walk night was going to and from the target. We'd hold hands, and Dad would ask questions and life would just fall out.

My dad learned about walks from Willy. When they first started hanging out they would walk to the hardware store together, or to buy film, stupid errands.

Most of the buildings on Morton Street had a single-pipe steam heat system.

Radiators in each room and a boiler in the basement. Steam would be made in the boiler and rise through a pipe that ran up the building.

A big problem the single-pipe system had was as the steam went up, its heat would be absorbed by the cold pipe. So by the time it got to the third or fourth floor, it wasn't so steamy anymore.

Sometimes it wasn't steam at all; it would be so cold that the steam condensed into water and dropped down, not heating the top floor at all.

This made the floors get progressively cooler, the higher they got.

It also made a racket. As the water (aka ex-steam) dripped down the pipe, it hit the new hot steam coming up. The water bounced off the steam, hitting the sides of the pipe like a pinball. But it didn't sound like pinball. It sounded like a crazy person banging on the pipe with a cast iron skillet.

If the system was going all the time, the pipes wouldn't get cold and it all worked well enough, though the first floor was always a sweatbox.

Landlords by law have to heat a building. In New York City the law was something like 68 degrees in the day and 55 degrees at night. So almost all boilers were on a timer to save money.

Because the pipes got cold each night, the single-pipe system almost never worked right.

Willy was the traveling super of number 40 on Morton Street, a six-story building with single-pipe heat. The apartment in the top floor was perpetually vacant.

Bullshit.

An empty apartment in New York City?

In the WEST VILLAGE?

Yes, this was way back. Before I was born. Before my dad knew Willy.

A musician named Charlie was broke and homeless. He and Willy were friends, so Willy let him live in the top floor of 40, and the apartment became perpetually occupied.

Winter rolls around and it is a bitter, awful cold.

It isn't the city's responsibility to clear the sidewalks of snow and ice. It is the property owners'. If an old lady falls because the walk is covered in ice, the landlord is held responsible for her broken hip.

But physically, it is the super's responsibility.

At the first hint of snow, a smart super gets out there and salts. If it is really bad the super only digs out a narrow path. Some supers only do paths. Willy always tried to do the whole sidewalk.

In addition to shoveling the walk, a super still needs to make sure the halls are clean.

And no matter how many scraps of cardboard you lay down in the entryway, the snow still gets dragged in and up the stairs.

Willy is cleaning the first floor of 40 when he hears shouting at him from the sixth floor.

It was a stair where you could see all the way up the center. Willy looks up and Charlie is hanging over the railing, screaming: "It's freezing. What you trying to do. Us poor black people are here trying to live and we ain't no Eskimos, we niggas!"

Willy said he would try to fix the problem.

The next day Willy introduced Charlie to a 45-year-old widow that lived across the street. She looked like *a minister's wife but with better tits.*

Charlie moved in with the minister's wife and the top apartment in 40 became perpetually vacant again.

By the time I was born, all the garbage can lids on Morton Street were chained to walls or fences. This was so they wouldn't fly away, get stolen, etc. If there were more than three inches of snow, Willy would unchain them for neighborhood kids.

Rome, Athens, and San Francisco boast seven hills. Greenwich Village had three. They were all located in Washington Square Park and were more like camel humps covered in asphalt.

In winter the humps were covered in snow and everyone under forty inches would sled down them on garbage can lids, crashing into the middle.

When summer came my sister and I would give each hump a belly flop hug. Face pressed to the warm asphalt, hoping no one skateboarded into us.

For a little while Willy ran a "whorehouse" on Morton Street. He was the traveling super of a big white brick building.

It was the first building on the block with an elevator and air conditioner sleeves below the windows. This made the rents higher, so there were always vacancies. Willy would fix up the empty apartments and rent them out to prostitutes.

He wasn't really a pimp, though he offered one of the girls to my dad. A beautiful one named Lucy who all you had to do to sleep with her was ask. My dad never asked her, but he was touched by the offer.

The first time my dad had jury duty he was selected to be on a liability case in civil court.

Jury duty in New York City today is a dream. Free Wi-Fi, snack breaks, and places to plug in a laptop. Civic pride radiates from the walls. Plus, if you are not picked to be on a jury, it is over in one or two days.

The first time I had jury duty I remember being thirsty and hungry, feeling threatened, confused, and that I was being punished for stealing plastic grapes.

When my dad served as a juror in 1968 it was worse. There was a popular joke: How can you expect justice from twelve people who can't even get out of jury duty?

On the first day of the case my dad took his place in the juror box, wearing chino slacks and a white button-down shirt.

A young black girl was suing the super of her building. She was small, no more than twelve.

The case was about an incident that had happened a few years before:

It was summertime in a slumlord building. The superintendent didn't like kids hanging around his turf, so he sprinkled plumber's lye on the stoop. The small girl sat on the stoop, not noticing the white powder. Water was thrown at her from an unknown source. The water mixed with the lye and splashed up and down her little back, burning and scarring her body.

The bailiff introduces the honorable Judge Crater, who starts the proceedings.

Judge Crater berates the little girl's lawyer for wearing a bow tie. Only neckties are allowed in his court. The trial will not continue unless this situation is resolved. The girl's lawyer leaves.

The lawyer returns wearing a necktie and the trial begins. Immediately the small girl is called to the stand. She speaks very softly. It is not a whisper; it is more she is scared to death.

"If you don't speak up, I am going to throw your case out of court," the judge screams at the girl.

So the girl speaks up, and does her best to stay loud, even as she must expose exhibit A to the courtroom. Exhibit A is her little naked scarred-up backside, including her bare ass.

The case goes on; they interview a few more people. It's time to go home, but the case isn't complete.

My dad leaves the courtroom. He is in the hallway waiting for the elevator. The bailiff comes out, calls him over, and says, "Judge Crater would like you to wear a suit tomorrow."

"Tell Judge Crater to go fuck himself," says my dad.

The elevator shows up, my dad gets in and leaves the building.

Outside, two cops stop him and bring him back upstairs to Judge Crater's court.

"You people all belong in jail," the judge screams, and then rants and raves about the Columbia riots.

The Columbia riots had just happened—mass protests against Columbia University's support of the Vietnam War and their plan to build a new gymnasium in a public park. The gym was to have a front entrance for students (mostly whites) and a back basement entrance for local residents (mostly blacks and hispanics). The students and citizens shut the university down for more than a week, taking over the whole campus, chanting "GYM CROW MUST GO" and "PEACE NOW."

"You will come here tomorrow dressed in a suit and tie or I will throw you in jail," Judge Crater threatens.

The next day my dad wore a raincoat buttoned to his Adam's apple.

Judge Crater starts the hearing. The judge keeps looking at my dad in the juror's box.

Crater is waiting for him to take off the raincoat. No way my dad is even undoing one button.

The case goes on. In the middle of an 11-year-old boy's testimony the judge halts the proceedings.

"Juror number one, did you wear a suit today?"

"May I have permission to speak freely, Your Honor?" my dad replies.

"No," says Judge Crater.

The bailiff is ordered to bring my dad to the front of the court and take his coat off.

A navy blue suit and necktie that my dad had borrowed from Willy is revealed.

"Escort this gentleman out of the building. I'm calling a mistrial," Judge Crater says, banging his gavel.

My dad didn't get called to do jury duty for twenty-five years.

But it bugged my dad, and he asked friends and strangers about the judge for months after the trial.

All supers are not created equal. Some are child molesters, and others are saints who make Plexiglas furniture in their spare time. Willy and my dad were cordial to all the supers in the neighborhood, but kept the bad ones at arm's length.

Agnes was the saint. She had graduated from Bennington and came from a wealthy family in Virginia. Always dressed in mechanic's overalls, she was the first lesbian my dad ever met. Agnes took great care of her building, but finally quit in disgust at what a complete prick the landlord was.

Ben was a class act from the Midwest. Ran his building like a ship. He had a nice ground-floor apartment, and a landlord that cared about the tenants. Ben had a string of capable assistants. The most capable of them all was a guy everyone called "Green."

Green would often join my dad and Willy on the stoop. He was young, but that's not why they called him Green.

Green was just his last name.

My dad truly loved him, and wondered why a good-looking, friendly, intelligent kid like that wasn't a doctor or a teacher. But he guessed it was 'cause Green was black and grew up poor.

Green had a wife named Noreen, though he couldn't have been more than 19. Noreen caught Green cheating on her, and she turned him in to the draft board.

Green was sent to Vietnam and they never saw him again.

It was around the time Green left when a locksmith found out that Judge Crater's son had been killed in Vietnam.

Tenants would sit on the stoop now and then, too. When this happened, Willy would talk about a neutral topic like what a motherfucker the landlord was, but mostly he just listened.

The first day my dad officially met Willy, they were walking down the street. A guy in a suit came up to Willy and asked, "Do you know Willoughby?"

Nope, never heard of him, Willy answered.

"Aren't you curious what he wanted?" my dad asked after the man left.

Nope.

If he was asked, "How you doing?" Willy would answer: *Fine.*

If he was asked, "What do you do for a living?" Willy would answer: *Things.*

Most of the neighborhood only knew what they saw of him: that he was a good mechanic who was tall and liked to sing while he put the cans out.

Some people might have noticed that he was sleeping with every woman on the block.

But Willy went out of his way to limit the "inter" of all his interactions.

It was funny, because Willy knew everything about everybody. My dad did, too.

Two doors down from Willy's stoop was a building filled with Russians.

The building was co-owned by a man named Patrick, who was the first American to sit on the board of Amnesty International, and a woman named Fran, whose husband was a famous industrialist that committed suicide.

The leftist and the capitalist's widow. The great buddy comedy that never was.

Almost every exiled Russian that came to America stayed at the buddy building. The Village was cheap and a good place to land.

Patrick was a professor of history. Russian history. But it was his Amnesty International connection that was the source of the Russians. They were all amazing.

It is hard to know how amazing these Russians were, because they spoke mostly Russian and my father did not.

Aleksandr Solzhenitsyn, Svetlana Stalin, Mikhail Baryshnikov, and Joseph Brodsky. These are names my dad knew from the many Russians that lived in the buddy building.

A girl named Rima lived there, too. Chunky, gracious, and polite, Rima had the power to take Americans to Russia. This was at a time when the only way you got there was on a guided Russian tour that had spies. No visas were given. It was an open secret that you could either go on the tour organized by the KGB or the tour organized by Rima.

Rima was best friends with a girl named Jenny, who was Llewellyn Thompson's daughter.

Llewellyn Thompson was the ambassador to the Soviet Union during the Cuban Missile Crisis. When the shit was hitting the fan, JFK received two messages from Nikita Khrushchev, one after the other. The first one was polite and diplomatic. The second was aggressive and threatening.

Llewellyn advised JFK to just answer the first message and pretend the second message didn't exist.

It worked. His suggestion maybe helped save the entire world, and it seems only fair that his daughter's best friend could go to Russia whenever she wanted.

Twenty stoops away from the buddy building, in 1957, the director of a Russian spy network was busted.

When the news broke out, everyone on the block was interviewed.

"Did you know he was a spy?" asked the reporter from one of New York's eight daily newspapers.
"Sure. Everyone knew that. No one cared," said Beatnik Bob from next door.
"Why?"
"This is the Village. There's commies, there's queers, there's blacks, we don't judge."

In order to send his secret messages, the spy needed to run a noisy generator. Because of the time difference, he sent his messages in the middle of the night.

This bothered his neighbors and they reported him to the FBI.

You can be anything you want in the Village, but don't keep people up at night.

MY JEWELS

Jason digs the sofa. It is mission style with leather cushions. He wants to sit on it, but is afraid.

We are at the writer and cartoonist James Thurber's historic house in Columbus, Ohio. A docent tells us it's okay to sit. We can even play the piano if we want. The house is original but has been re-furnished in the style of 1913–1917, when Thurber lived here.

A clock sits on the mantel, a candlestick phone on the sideboard, and lace doilies under bowls. They have done a good job, but no one more so than the person who did the wallpaper.

The tour is free and self-guided. To start, we watch a video that runs on a loop in the dining room.

There is archival footage of Thurber. He talks about his cartoons being rejected fifteen times by *The New Yorker*, and tells how the writer E. B. White stuck up for him. This means E. B. White gets a shout-out from Thurber thirty, possibly forty times a day. *The New Yorker* went on to publish hundreds of Thurber's drawings.

We go up the same stairs Thurber's aunt threw shoes down. She did this at night to scare off imaginary burglars.

Thurber's actual typewriter sits under a gooseneck lamp. The last thing he typed was "Please. Do Not Touch."

Another item that really belonged to Thurber: his magnifying loupe. It is placed in front of a photo so we know what the thing is. The photo is of Thurber wearing the loupe drawing a cartoon. He is two inches away from the paper.

When Thurber was a kid he lost an eye playing "William Tell" with his brother.

I don't know how much being half-blind affected Thurber's drawings. The film explained one of the reasons he was first rejected by *The New Yorker* was his drawing of a seal did not look like a seal. E. B. White argued that a Thurber seal was better than a real one.

E. B. White did more than argue; he pulled Thurber's drawings out of the trash. Recognizing value where others had not. He fought to make people understand that though the work was crude, it was special. And he won.

We stop at a wall of autographed eight-by-ten photos. They are writers that once had residencies here. Our favorite is a guy whose name we can't make out because he has signed his face.

Next to the kitchen is the gift shop. I ask the cashier where we can find the "These Are My Jewels" statue. She is polite but has no idea.

The statue is from a chapter in *My Life and Hard Times*. Columbus gets hit by an imaginary flood. A woman, trying to escape, climbs the town's Civil War monument. "These Are My Jewels" is inscribed on the statue. Thurber drew a cartoon of the woman on top of the bronze soldiers who watch "with cold unconcern." She wasn't naked in the story but is in the cartoon.

"Maybe it's by a courthouse?" Jason asks.
"That could be. It's worth a try," the cashier says.

Drawing by James Thurber from "The Day the Dam Broke"

The center of downtown: Sherman, Stanton, Grant, and Sheridan are there as described. So is the phrase "These Are My Jewels." But instead of an empty pedestal above them, there is a sculpture of a lady. She isn't naked, but you can see nipples through her dress. I look up and think about how back at the house, Thurber is probably saying nice things about E. B. White right now.

GATEWAY DRUG

Clue: Game changer Farrar?

Straight out of college, Margaret Petherbridge got a job as a secretary to the Sunday editor of the *New York World*.

This was 1919.

It wasn't part of her job description, but one of Margaret's duties was helping Arthur Wynne edit the Sunday crossword puzzle.

The first crossword puzzle was actually published by the *New York World* in 1913. It was created by Arthur Wynne and was labeled "Word-Cross Puzzle."

A few weeks later the typesetters messed up and set the title as "Cross-Word Puzzle."

So when Margaret went to work, crosswords were a new thing. *The New York Times* looked down its nose at them. Other papers just thought they were too much work.

Even the *New York World* thought the puzzles weren't worth the trouble and tried to stop printing them, but the readers revolted, threatening to switch to one of the twenty-five other New York daily papers (none of which had crossword puzzles).

As it turns out, Margaret was put on this earth to edit crossword puzzles. Little by little, she improved the structure and rules. She wasn't trying to make the puzzles harder; she was trying to make them more enjoyable. The clues got less dry, the grids more attractive, and the challenges more satisfying.

Around this time Richard L. Simon had an aunt that was hooked on the *New York World*'s crossword puzzles. She asked him to find her a book of just crosswords. Richard found such a book didn't exist, so he decided to make one with his partner, Max Schuster.

They asked Margaret to help.

The Cross-Word-Puzzle Book came out in 1924 with a pencil attached as a sales gimmick. It was the first book of crosswords ever printed.

People caught puzzle fever. Dictionary and thesaurus sales rose. Library encyclopedias got a workout. Everyone all the sudden knew what a gnu was. And Simon & Schuster overnight became a major publisher.

Hundreds of thousands of *The Cross-Word-Puzzle Book* sold within the first year.

More crossword books by Margaret followed. Checkered clothes became popular, and newspapers across the country were forced to carry crossword puzzles.

Except *The New York Times*, which called them a "primitive mental exercise" and feared the crossword would be a gateway drug to comics.

Then World War II hit. A memo was sent around *The New York Times* offices suggesting that crossword puzzles be added to the paper. The Sunday editor thought it would give people something to do if there were blackout hours, and might help lighten people's mood.

The memo included a correspondence with Margaret, who had been contacted for advice.

> The Herald Tribune runs the best puzzle page in existence so far, but they have gotten into a bit of a rut. Their big puzzle never ventures even one imaginative definition, and lacks the plus quality that I believe can be achieved and maintained . . . We could, I dare to predict, get the edge on them with the above plan.

The above plan was to have "meat and dessert" on the Sunday page. A challenging puzzle that gave "real satisfaction," plus a smaller, more humorous puzzle that acted as the banana split.

Arthur Hays Sulzberger was the owner and final decision maker of *The New York Times*. He loved crossword puzzles and was sick of buying the *Herald Tribune*.

Margaret was hired as the editor, and the first *New York Times* crossword puzzle ran February 15, 1942.

A puzzle editor doesn't construct the puzzles. The puzzles are sent in by hobbyists. This situation was set up by Arthur Wynne from nearly the get-go. People wrote to him criticizing his first puzzles, saying that they could make a better puzzle. Go right ahead, I dare you, was Wynne's response, saving himself a ton of work.

Margaret's job was to set rules, make the puzzle the right difficulty, check facts, add life, and find great puzzle constructors.

She assembled a Delta Force of elite puzzle constructors that were brilliant and poetic. Her rules weeded out any mediocre grids, and from its beginning the *New York Times* puzzle was seen as the best.

Every source I've read calls her a "puzzle pioneer." At a time when women all over the country were giving their jobs back to men, Margaret was kicking ass.

In 1926 Margaret married John C. Farrar, one of the founders of the Farrar, Straus and Giroux publishing house. John was born in Vermont, went to Yale, spoke out against censorship, and published the writer Flannery O'Connor.

I bring John up because from what I've read he was a great man and the least talked-about letter of FSG, but mostly because Margaret's last name changed to Farrar.

Margaret Farrar's Delta Force of puzzle constructors came from all walks of life: musicians, prisoners, sea captains.

And high school students.

My dad would call Margaret up directly. She would explain that a person of good intelligence should be able to finish the puzzle in the time it takes to get from Scarsdale to New York City.

The first *New York Times* crossword puzzle constructed by my dad was printed in 1959 while he was a senior at White Plains High School.

Kenneth Henry Shopsin (my father) was born 1942, in the Bronx. His father, Morris, owned a paper factory with his brother, Sydney, that was located on Vandam Street in downtown Manhattan.

As a kid my dad would get beat up for being Jewish. His neighborhood in the Bronx was mainly Irish, Italian, and racist.

When my dad was 12, black people started to move into the neighborhood. My grandpa Morris wanted to leave right away. Not because he was racist. Because he was a Jew. He knew his property value was going to go down.

But he waited for two or three years to sell. He didn't want to be the first one on the block to sell to black people. He didn't want the neighbors to say, "Ah, those fucking Jews, they will do anything for money."

Morris came home one day with a big smile. He had learned that the Irish guy three doors down had sold to blacks, which gave him permission to sell to blacks, too.

The Shopsins moved to White Plains, New York, a few blocks from the border of Scarsdale.

In summer my dad regularly took the train down to work at the paper factory.

He ended up on the same schedule as a man named Bill.

Bill was an executive at Union Carbide that was three times my dad's age, with a wife, two kids, and an office designed by Skidmore, Owings & Merrill. He wore a suit and did the *New York Times* crossword puzzle every day.

One day Bill and my dad did the puzzle together, and they both had a great time. From then on my dad and Bill found each other on the Metro North platform each morning, pencils in hand.

They would celebrate each victory together by crumpling up the completed crossword and throwing it in the trash.

When summer ended, my dad started doing the puzzles alone. Which sounds sad, but it wasn't. He had found a passion.

My dad met Margaret by mail when he ordered some puzzle constructor paper with a preprinted grid. He didn't use the paper the way you were supposed to. The way my dad made puzzles was he just took old puzzles and filled them in with new words and clues. Then he copied the puzzle onto the special paper.

Margaret's telephone number came with the special paper.

The number came with the constructor paper because there are a shit ton of rules to construct a *New York Times* puzzle. Rules that were all created by Margaret. Maximum % of black squares, diametrically symmetrical, slang is okay, obscure words are not, you can't use clues that have been used before ("repeaters"), no diseases allowed, and on and on.

The puzzle fever had long died down. Bridge was now king. There couldn't have been more than a hundred or two constructors. My dad was paid fifteen dollars a puzzle, more for a Sunday puzzle, but not much.

There is a twinkle when my dad remembers Margaret. He never met her in person, but all the puzzles she rejected or accepted came with a full-page letter and annotated clues.

"You could just call her anytime?" I asked my dad.

"No one else must have called her. She always answered right away. What a sweet lady," my dad says, and tells me he has an embroidered pillow his mom made with the last puzzle he ever constructed.

The puzzle was published a few months before Margaret retired.

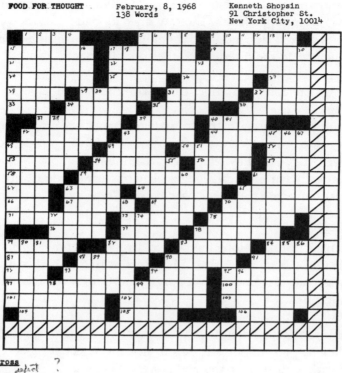

Across

1. Eye: Comb. form.
5. Wave: Fr.
9. Forgo, as a dance.
15. Military posture.
17. Shoot.
19. Noodle soup with beef, Korean style.
21. Woman of the year: slang.
22. Borscht circuit delicacy.
24. Swabs.
25. "...our trespasses---..."
26. --- ease.
27. Booking agent letters.
28. Spread.
29. --- the good.
31. Diets.
32. False god.
33. Indian weight.
34. Old womanish.
35. One of twelve.
36. Oriental weights.
37. Oil extracts.
39. One of two.
40. Feel dizzy.
42. Football term.
43. "--- good egg."
44. Specimen.
48. Supplication to the hunt godess.
49. Biblical pronoun.
50. "Grapes of Wrath."
52. Duck genus.
53. Compound prefix.
54. Intones.
56. Cape.
57. Resole.
58. Monkshood.
59. Arabian meat balls.
61. Italian painter.

Across

62. Familiar form of address.
63. Contrary gardener.
64. Trial.
65. Ritual feast.
66. Caucasian Moslem.
67. Surface measures.
69. Frommage, Hollandaise.
70. Olive mate.
71. Empowers.
73. Stripes.
75. Themes.
76. Affixes.
77. Plato's "Ideas."
78. --- pot.
79. Dodgson girl.
82. Cysts.
83. Market factor.
84. "Y" rule product.
87. Stone monument.
88. Gravy craft.
90. --- phrase.
91. Whiskers.
92. "---little teapot..."
93. Whale man a la Douay.
94. Fillet.
95. Hunting dog.
97. Omened pastries.
100. Drew close.
101. Surly one.
102. Turmoil.
103. Pied paper.
104. Hamburgers on the hoof.
105. Pothole holder.
106. Platinum loop.

Down

1. Actor Peter.
2. Neopolitan treat.
3. Declarative retort.
4. Small amount.
5. One---.
6. Headland.
7. Musical group.
8. Addis Ababa cuisine.
9. Norse poet.
10. Namesakes of Eurytus' daughter.
11. Balsam.
12. Approves.
13. Hope at Christmas.
14. Central American bird.
15. Vapor: Gr.
16. Spanish meat pie.
17. Sizes.
18. Anchovy form.
20. Gems.
23. Backgammon term.
30. To read: Fr.
31. Competitive meet: Ir.
32. Ointment.
34. One of four, usually.
35. Lamb dish.
36. Messes.
38. Nicholas and Ivan.
39. --- we eat?
40. Divulge.
41. X,S.
42. Partial poem title.
43. ---Hing, Chinese city.
45. French delight.
46. Not ringers.
47. Termination.
48. Answer man.
49. Evergreen.
51. Sometime swiss location
54. Coddle.
55. Venison cut.
59. Ventured.
60. Seven of seven.
61. Second fired.
63. ---mer.
65. Italian numeral.
68. Sauce words.
70. Chili, Mexican style.
72. Music man.
74. Ones: Ger.
75. Chinese noodles.
78. Most askew.
79. Arabic ones.
80. "C" source.
81. Minor diamond.
82. Military acronym.
83. Anode and cathode.
85. Two summers in France.
86. Carnelian: Lat.
88. Fish man.
89. Heavy blows.
90. Waxed lachrymose.
91. Grab.
93. Woman's nickname.
94. Gumbo.
96. Gaseous prefix.
98. Town: Cornish prefix.
99. Biblical name.

See page 323 for answers. FYI: Puzzle is unedited.

February 17th, 1968

Dear Mr. Shopsin:

I finally found time to give this one a try, and I admire your style and ingenuity. But -- I must conclude that you are taking too many liberties with good form -- at least for the Times page where we are dedicated to the traditional rules. I know we've been resorting to some trickery recently, and we hear about it from many a solver. I know we'll never please everybody, but we're expected to hold the fort on the rules -- otherwise chaos may ensue.

The phrase rule, for example, is important -- made-up phrases to fill the constructor's need are not welcome. And we don't want to stoop to the 2-wd., 3 wd. hints.

I am sorry to return because well I know the time and cogitation that go into these constructions.. See some notes and queries on your words and defs. I have your Daily puzzle around and hope to get to it soon, have your note about it.

I shouldn't issue invitations to come again because the file is full to overflowing, but I'd be happy to have you -- think you'll land if you'll take all those rules, and watch out for the impossible crossings, etc. etc.

Yours sincerely,

Margaret Farrar

132

When my dad moved to the Village, his first apartment was on Christopher Street. Margaret Farrar was still the puzzle editor. Every night he would go to the Riker's near his home at 10:15 p.m., when the late edition of *The New York Times* came out.

Riker's was a chain of twenty-four-hour coffee shops. The one near my dad had a guy named Garry that ran the night shift. Garry was straitlaced, likely had a wife at home and went to church on Sundays.

But Garry loved transvestites. A large crew of them would come in and hang out. Garry would treat them special.

Not in a creepy sex-for-donut way. He just dug them and learned their names.

So my dad was there every night. Ostensibly to do the crossword puzzle, but also because he really liked the place and the mixed crowd that hung out there.

Eventually he met a guy named Roger that made his living as a perfume expert. They started doing the puzzle together every night.

Roger introduced my dad to Albert Donati. Albert was two decades older with big muscles and an anchor tattoo. Despite these differences, my dad and Albert got to be close friends.

Albert is the one that told my dad about being a super and set him up with his first building.

4●   3●

2
●

●1

5 ●

8●   ●9

6●   7●

Albert was a sailor. Well, he had once been a sailor.

He got very active in the sailors' union, the NMU (National Maritime Union).

Then he had a falling-out with the union's leader. A guy named Joseph Curran. And the way Curran dealt with people that gave him a problem was to report said person to the FBI as a communist.

And poof, Albert wasn't a sailor anymore.

In fact, Albert was a communist. But that is beside the point.

> Almost everyone in the 1930s and 1940s was a communist.
> —my dad

Every job Albert had after the NMU, two guys in fedoras would show up and flash badges to his boss. The two guys would say, "Did you know you're employing a communist?"

The FBI paid agents a salary to go around and do that. They did it to Albert for twenty years.

Albert loved it.

Because:

1. Most of the people he worked for were commies anyway.

2. He had so plainly lost the fight, but that they still considered him an enemy made him feel good.

A woman named Ilsa walked fast and worked nights as an elite typist. My dad says her daughter, Nora, was the best-behaved kid he ever saw.

I don't think he meant this as a compliment.

Nora played violin and went to Our Lady of Pompeii on Bleecker Street. She wore the same uniform as everyone else, plaid skirt and knee socks—but she wore it better.

Not better as in cool kid with upturned collar; better as in more historic. Like a perfect black-and-white photo of a European schoolgirl taken in front of the Alps.

Ilsa was born and raised in Switzerland. She was the star of that historic photo. Most of her free time was spent taking Nora to recitals and practice. They both were always neat and put together.

Before Morton Street, Ilsa had lived on Ibiza. I don't know what she did there. Likely worked as a laser-accurate typist. On Morton Street she lived next to the buddy building.

Her building had a problem with cockroaches.

It happens.

An exterminator was called, and everyone's problem was fixed. Except Ilsa's.

She kept complaining, but nobody else had the problem anymore.

So the exterminator goes back to her apartment.

It is spotless, hands-and-knees clean.

The exterminator looks at all the places he put the spray for the roaches. They are all gleaming. You could lick the corners and cabinets without a worry, and that is just what the bugs were doing.

Ilsa had scrubbed all the poison off as soon as the exterminator left.

The first time my dad bought drugs was from a guy named Junior that had lived on the block all his life. Junior was Italian, connected with the Mafia, and he pronounced "Jewish" as "Jooich."

When my dad went to pay, Junior starts screaming:

"What are you, fucking stupid? I'm a drug dealer, you gonna pay me by check? You got rocks in your head?"

Junior starts to kick the shit out of my dad.

Willy walks by and pulls Junior off my dad like he was a piece of lint.

Willy didn't drink or smoke, but when he did one he did the other.

He'd bum cigarettes off my dad, but never bought them because he didn't smoke.

But after a scotch or two he did.

When Willy wanted to lose weight, he would buy a big can of cheap sardines. Then he'd make a rule that for two days all he could eat was sardine sandwiches.

Halfway through the first sandwich, Willy would get disgusted and lose his appetite for two days.

There were lots of things like that with Willy. He would let himself drift, and then pull himself back to what he considered to be the right place.

Cap'n Jack was a super you kept at arm's length. He took care of an insane amount of buildings.

Any more than four buildings at a time was insane to my dad and Willy. The whole point of being a super was to not work.

You had to deal with the garbage and mopping the halls. Once you went over four buildings it was like you had a real job. And if you were willing to have a real job, there were a lot better ways to make money.

Cap'n Jack took care of twenty or thirty buildings, but this isn't what made him seem insane.

Mostly it was the smell.

He always had on the same outfit that he wore till it fell apart. Lots of denim and fur. It seemed more like two outfits than one. He never washed his clothes, and never bathed, though part of his outfit was a shower cap.

Wearing his shower cap as a blindfold, Cap'n Jack's hands were always full like Lady Justice's. In one hand he carried a scratched-up cane, and in the other was a plastic bag full of plastic bags. Symbolizing not justice and objectivity, but what a total whack job he was.

Cap'n worked hard. Too hard. His buildings were not just little brownstones but big co-ops with a hundred tenants. He made a lot of money being a super.

But Cap'n didn't really spend money on anything. Certainly not his clothes. And he had a rent-controlled apartment. Which is like an R.S. apartment but five hundred times better. The rent never goes up and the only way to evict you is if you die.

Some New Yorkers have borne children just to pass down their R.C. apartments. As though the R.C. apartment is an eternal flame that will let them live on in proxy.

My dad knew a guy named Nick that had a sweet R.C. apartment on Barrow Street.

$135 a month, forever.

During World War II Nick had developed the technology that paved the way for whipped cream in a can. He made his first fortune by inventing automated baking machines.

The machines turned out hundreds of loaves and rolls a minute, and destroyed the traditional baking industry.

Nick made his second fortune with spray foam. The type you use for home insulation.

Armstrong, and lots of other brands, had been in the industry for a while. But it was discovered that the formulas they were using caused cancer.

Somehow aware of this, Nick had bought the rights to the one spray foam formula that was noncarcinogenic. He discovered, along the way, the same foam with some dye in it was a good way to mail seedlings.

And that was how Nick made his third fortune.

He had a huge house in Westchester, but kept the R.C. apartment all his life. His daughter may still have the place.

The list of rich and rent-controlled is long. BFD.

Plenty of people truly needed their R.C. and R.S. apartments. Scrappy orphans, single mothers, poets, seniors, and nutso couples that had five kids.

But there was a flip side to R.S. and R.C. apartments. You got trapped by the low rent and never bought your own piece of New York.

Whatever the faults, R.C. and R.S. kept the Village diverse with a banker, baker, and candlestick maker all on one floor.

It wasn't a perfect system. But neither is life.

At some point, property sharks started buying all the buildings in the Village. Emptying them of working-class and poor tenants, bending the rent stabilization laws till they broke.

The sharks then either flipped the buildings for an instant profit or ran them as cash machines, raising the rents up and down the block.

And the Village changed. Some people think it's better. You can lick the corners and cabinets of it without a worry.

But that hadn't happened yet.

The fringe people still found a home on Morton Street.

A GIFT

When it snowed, Cap'n Jack would be fucked. So he would hire Willy to shovel half his walks. My dad would always be pulled in to help.

They cleared the walks for extra cash, but also because Cap'n Jack was part of the block, and he was drowning.

Besides, if his walks didn't get shoveled and salted, no one could get down the street.

People looked out for each other even if it was a pain in the ass. This might have been because the Village was more dangerous and hardscrabble, because people lived there longer, were in more need, or just talked to each other more.

Note: I wasn't born yet.

Plenty of fucked-up shit went on. There was a gang of boys that lived on Eleventh Street who would beat up black people for fun. Drug addicts sleeping the day away. Homeless people living in children's playgrounds. The smell of piss on the street. It is easy to cite the bad in the filthy chaos of New York before luxury condos. It is harder to express the spirit, life, and community that the chaos and inefficiency bred.

Mr. King Kong, this is your last warning:
YOU MUST HAVE A TICKET

On top of this, things were still made in NYC. The cost of rent for workers and businesses was lower, so paper factories dotted Tribeca. Garments were made in the Garment District, and *The New York Times* was printed in the New York Times Building near Times Square.

The transistor was invented in the West Village at the Bell Labs Building on Bethune Street. Lots of things were invented there under the umbrella of improving telephone service. Amplifiers, vacuum tubes, solar panels, etc. And during the world wars, the labs helped perfect radar and other essential military electronics like voice scramblers.

But if the only thing that ever came out of the huge building with the freight train running through it was the transistor, that would be plenty.

My dad had a best friend called Casko that lived on Morton Street. He had a wife named Jean, kids, and a Chevrolet Corvair that he was always fixing. Willy wasn't my dad's best friend; they were more like a married couple.

Willy's best friend was Memphis.

Memphis was a mythical scarred-up tough with a pilot's license and a vicious dog. Memphis's dog knew not to bark at my dad, and Casko got an X-rated Christmas card from Willy once, but for the most part their friends didn't mix.

Casko was an engineer, hired in the last days of the Bethune Street Bell Labs. Weeks after he was hired, the whole operation moved to a new compound in Holmdel, New Jersey. Casko would commute daily by motorcycle to program giant computers and work on defense contracts.

My dad says Casko was calculating missile trajectories. I've never heard these words come out of Casko's mouth. He doesn't talk about it so much, but he did tell me he was at a party on the block once when a hip lady asked what he did for a living. Casko answered that he "worked on defense technologies." The woman said, "That's a shame, man," and walked away.

Don't keep your neighbors up; don't work for the army. Other than that, a very tolerant place.

Cap'n Jack would offer Casko clothes from the garbage. The clothes were almost brand-new. They came from the condos Cap'n took care of. He would comb an insane amount of trash before he put it out on the street. Cap'n would then give his finds away to anyone in his path.

"I didn't know he was a pervert. Jean did. She never let him near the kids. She had a feeling about stuff like that," Casko once told me.

It took my dad and Willy ten years to know.

They maybe kind of knew before. There were lots of lowlifes, and in the scheme of things Cap'n didn't seem that bad.

But one day they are all on the stoop when Cap'n expresses his interest in a close friend's 8-year-old daughter.

Disgust sets in.

"That is weird. You are going to get arrested and go to jail," my dad says to Cap'n. Cap'n sort of shrugs and changes the topic.

They still shoveled Cap'n Jack's walks. They still said "hello," but they blocked him from the girl, and they warned anyone who had a daughter.

My dad was working part-time in the Church Street Post Office twenty hours a week. The part-time employees there were all kind of broken. He made friends with one named Frank.

Frank had a day job at a designer fabric store on Broadway. He was a compulsive gambler that was always being threatened by someone he owed money to.

Dad made the mistake of lending Frank a hundred dollars. He did this so Frank wouldn't get beat up.

Finally my dad got angry and told Frank it was time to pay him back. It wasn't right; he had helped him out of a jam. Frank says, come see me at work.

My dad goes over to Broadway. This is when there were factories above and textile stores up and down the block near Canal Street.

Frank's shop is fancy, with high ceilings, plaster details, and bolts of fabric as far as the eye can see.

Dad goes to the counter; Frank wraps something up and writes out a slip. He hands it to my dad and says, "Now we are even."

When my dad unwrapped the package at home he found a brocade bedspread in gold and red. Similar to the Unicorn Tapestries at the Cloisters but with tassels. It must have been worth a fortune, but my dad had no use for it. So he gave it to Willy and just called it even with Frank.

A month later my dad asked, "Hey, Willy, how you like the bed-spread?

Great, I sold it. Got a hundred and a quarter for it.
"I gave that to you as a gift."
You know what a gift is?
"What?"
When you give it to somebody it's theirs. I used it how I wanted to use it.
My dad accepted that.

Dad didn't give a shit about the blanket in the first place, and in the end it was worth the hundred bucks to give Willy the joy of putting one over.

Willy deserved that happiness. He always took care of his tenants no matter what a piece of work they were. There was a team of elderly people Willy brought food and newspapers to. This was before the rise of restaurant delivery and the Internet. If someone got sick, he visited them in the hospital and brought them their mail.

It was hard to really know Willy but it was easy to know his good parts.

When Memphis went to prison, he asked Willy to watch his German shepherd, whose name was Mother Fucker. "No problem," said Willy to taking care of the meanest dog in Manhattan.

Willy fell in love with Mother Fucker.

They went everywhere together, and within a week he had changed the dog into a softie named Mickey. He just was so kind to the dog it forgot how to be a motherfucker.

When Memphis finally got out of jail, Willy didn't want to give Mickey back, but he knew he had to.

Memphis took one look at Mickey and said he wanted nothing to do with a pussy dog like that.

Willy and Mickey lived together happily ever after.

Except years later, a Doberman was being a dick at the park. Went after a poodle or something. Whatever it did, Mickey snapped and turned back into Mother Fucker and killed the Doberman.

I don't know the details, but the next week Mickey died. The owner of the Doberman had somehow poisoned Mickey.

Mickey being poisoned was the only story Willy ever told in the basement that made him cry.

Cap'n Jack was sick in the hospital.

Willy went to see him.

Why did he go see a pervert? To talk about covering his super work. To say he could not cover Jack's buildings. To bring him some mail or news. Pick one. They are all likely true. Even if he was a pervert, Cap'n was the neighborhood pervert and Willy cared about the neighborhood.

Miserable Jack. The nurses had bathed him and taken away his shower cap. He misses his routines and hates being clean. He starts to weep and cry that he wants to die.

Jack whispers to Willy, "Kill me."

No fucking way, Willy replies.

"There is eighty thousand dollars in cash hidden in my apartment. Kill me and it is yours."

You ain't got that money. Prove it.

Jack gave Willy the keys to his apartment.

Willy and my dad are walking. They have been walking for a while.

Kenny, Willy says.

"Yes, Will," my father answers.

Words start falling out.

In Jack's pigsty of an apartment there is eighty thousand dollars hidden under the mattress.

Jack is on death's door.

If it were Willy, he would want to die as well. Jack is no good, nobody is going to miss the sick fuck.

What would a pastor say? Maybe put it all in the tithe tray.

My dad just listens. He didn't say what to do.

He never told Willy what to do.

The conversation in my dad's memory doesn't seem like a big deal. He let Willy bounce shit off him all the time.

On the next walk my dad and Willy took there were less words, but they poured out the same.

Willy had killed Cap'n Jack in the hospital, and put all the money in the bank.

Nobody ever found out about the "whorehouse" Willy ran. Apartments in the Village became more valuable, and the landlord of the white brick building had no trouble renting them all out.

The building needed a live-in super, so one named Rosemary was hired to replace Willy. She lived there with her husband, Bruce.

Bruce had been a fighter pilot in the Korean War. Flew a P-51 Mustang and had been celebrated in adventure magazines, but now Bruce could hardly navigate across the street. He was a mess with big square feet that looked like he forgot to take the shoes out of the box.

Rosemary met Bruce at a bar. They were the last ones there. It wasn't love at first sight. Rosemary was getting old, and her clock was ticking. So they married and Rosemary got her baby, but Bruce was a drinker and it was only getting worse.

It's not fair to sum them up that way. In the limits of a situation there is humor, there is grace, and everything else.

Above Rosemary and Bruce lived a short, Satanic-looking drunk named Raymond and his girl, Eve.

Eve was barely twenty but had a good full-time job with vacation days.

Rosemary decided my dad would be a better match for Eve than Raymond. Eve agreed.

Rosemary knew my dad from the super circuit. She knew he had a part-time job at the post office and had hung out with him just enough to know he liked diet pink grapefruit soda.

Rosemary invited my dad to a poker game, and when he arrived, there was Eve, drinking a diet pink-grapefruit soda. But Eve was living with Raymond. So that was that.

In the middle of the night there was a ring at my dad's bell.

It's Eve. She is crying but also pissed off. She vows that Raymond has beaten her up for the last time.

The bell rings again. My dad's apartment was on the ground floor. He and Eve could see it was Raymond outside. Raymond starts to lean on the buzzer. My dad grabs his gun and tucks it in the back of his pants along his butt crack.

Dad won't let Raymond go past the vestibule.

"Sorry, Ray, Eve says she is not going back, ever," my dad warns.

Raymond left without a to-do, pretty much just accepted it and walked it off.

The next day on the stoop my dad gave Willy the rundown.

Willy looked my dad in the eye and said: *Wow, you're gonna go and have the whole catastrophe, aren't you?*

WHOOP WHOOP

A lighted sign says "Hi" as we turn in.

There are sticker machines and a security guard. It is almost midnight. We have just returned from a photo job in Paris.

Paris, Missouri.

A sweet girl behind the counter asks what we want. Eight things are on the menu.

I tell her we need more time.

We flew in last night.

At 6:30 this morning Jason was using a do-it-yourself waffle maker in the hotel's breakfast room while I picked out a road that wasn't too big or small.

It was three hours to Paris. The drive was perfect, with a peacock made of hay bales and a clapboard house decorated with a mysterious "E."

When the drive got boring, I read a manuscript aloud in preparation for the job.

The job was to make photos for a book cover of a memoir. A memoir about a man who returns home from a big city to the small town he grew up in. He returns to take care of his aging mother, Betty, who is struggling with dementia.

The man's name was George. He was very nice and greeted us at the door offering fruit salad.

It was a ranch home with freshly vacuumed carpet.

Betty was 92 but looked much younger, maybe 80 or 82. She didn't notice Jason and me till George introduced us.

The only portrait Jason had to take was the back of Betty as she played the piano. That was the first of two setup images Jason needed to nail or the art director might get fired. A still life of a dresser was the other.

George was nervous about the piano shot. He'd only told Betty he wrote the book a few days ago.

We did the still life first.

It was not so still, because it involved a dog named Raj that scared the crap out of me.

Books were stacked waist high. George explained the books were all his; there was not a lot to do in Paris on Saturday nights.

I asked if a big mirror above the piano could be moved. This was so that there would be a clean area in the photo for the designer to place text.

"Betty is not going to like this," George said as he helped us move the mirror.

Jason framed the shot. I acted as Betty's stand-in and pretended to play the piano.

Before Betty even entered the room she wanted to know where the mirror was.

I clapped. It seemed a magic trick for Betty to play the piano like that. Jason nodded at me, and I knew the art director would not get fired.

George drove us toward Main Street, pointing out places that were mentioned in his book.

He also pointed out the meth houses, explained that sheets as curtains was a sure sign of drugs, and that the only sign surer was a blown-off roof.

The land that surrounded Paris was once full of small family farms. All the farms are now owned by one company. This is one of many reasons Paris's Main Street is dying.

George was 8 when his family decided to move away from his birthplace of Madison, Missouri. He was excited, hoping for Chicago, San Francisco, or St. Louis. His family moved fifteen miles up the road to Paris.

"You are very lucky," George told me when he heard I was born in New York City.

"There are roughly three New Yorks," E. B. White wrote in "Here Is New York," an essay written with so much love and grace its words become fact.

> There is, first, the New York of the man or woman who was born here, who takes the city for granted and accepts its size and its turbulence as natural and inevitable. Second, there is the New York of the commuter—the city that is devoured by locusts each day and spat out each night. Third, there is the New York of the person who was born somewhere else and came to New York in quest of something. Of these trembling cities the greatest is the last—the city of final destination, the city that is a goal. It is this third city that accounts for New York's high strung disposition, its poetical deportment, its dedication to the arts, and its incomparable achievements.

White failed to mention that the third New Yorker, the non-native, takes a thing for granted, too. The third New Yorker knows they can live somewhere else. They have done it once, deep down if need be they can do it again.

The first New Yorker has no such reservoir.

On the way back from lunch George gave a kind of soft pitch for us to move to Paris. You could buy a nice house for 40K, food was cheap, the sky was beautiful.

Boy, oh boy, I can't wait to get to dee Big Apple!

Jason decided we should book it back to Kansas City. This had nothing to do with the lack of humans in Paris. It had to do with the lack of BBQ.

We took the interstate.

Our order is up.

Jason and I start to go left. The checkout lady tells us the dining room is to the right. We come to a sauce bar with plastic soufflé cups. Beside it is a beverage station that has free water and coffee. A sign asks: "Please DO NOT use coffee cups FOR SAUCE."

"I like my coffee black," Jason says in a robot voice.
"I lyke mah coffee blaghk," I say back at him.

Low light from a wagon wheel chandelier sets the mood.

A waitress passes by, looks at Jason's plate, and makes the most sincere "mmm" I've ever heard.

Jason is impressed; she works here every day and still feels that way.

He is less impressed after he starts to eat.

When Jason was 24 he had a job designing video boxes for soft-core porn films. Tired of Photoshopping strategic shadows onto lesbian vampires, he quit and took his camera on a long motorcycle trip. He traveled down the Mississippi River guided by gas station maps.

Upon entering Kansas City, he found an overlook with a view of an industrial area known as "West Bottoms."

West Bottoms was full of warehouses and crisscrossed with train tracks. Jason was drawn to it and drove down to see if he could find a café.

He parked his motorcycle in front of an old factory. A man yelled from a window above, "What are you doing?" Jason looked up and shouted, "Just looking around."
"Do you want a coffee?" the man called back.

The man was named Davin and was the same age as Jason. His apartment was a crumbling brick semi-fixed-up loft. It was similar to one that Jason lived in back in Brooklyn, except Davin had the whole three-story building, and there had been a fire, so half a floor was missing.

The loft was Jason's fantasy come true, complete with a pack of roommates that didn't mind him crashing on the couch.

The couch felt good. Jason had been on the road for a while. Each morning he would wake up and decide to stay one more day.

All the roommates had jobs, but they worked on different days. So every day Jason got to hang out with a different roommate.

Roommate #1, Harriet, took him to see the Alligator Lady.

Alligator Lady was a black sheep of a wealthy family.

Her house was a big Victorian with ornate wood moldings, patterned wallpaper, and floors rimmed with green garden hoses. Every room had a filing cabinet, and a big cage.

In the filing cabinet were Xeroxes of articles and evidence against water fluoridation. In the cages were live alligators that the A.L. would carefully hose down. Interns from the local art school floated in and out of the rooms with freshly cut trays of dead chickens.

Roommate #2, Neal, took Jason to a record shop and introduced him to Hasil Adkins.

Roommate #3, Leo, took Jason to a BBQ place.

Actually, Jason took Leo to the BBQ place.

Leo couldn't explain how to get to it, just that it was worth the trip.

So Jason had Leo get on the back of his motorcycle, and the way you find a light switch in the dark, they found the BBQ place.

The light revealed a run-down gas station with a smoker whose doors had welded-on the initials "LC," junkyard style. When the doors opened, half a foot of black crust was baked to them, and inside were shelves of sweet meat.

Jason went back to the place the next two days so he would never forget where it was.

This is not that place. That place closed two hours ago.

We will go there tomorrow.

This is my second time in Kansas City. The first time was also with Jason. We drove in very late at night.

The first thing he did was take me to the West Bottoms overlook.

Snow on the ground and visible breath, I got out to join him.
"Whoop whoop," I said, universal code for please lock the car door.
"We don't need to. There is no one here. Come on," Jason answered.
"Whoop whoop."
"It's fine. We'll be here for ten seconds."
"Whoop whoop."
"It's silly. It is just over this wall. Come on, I want to show you."
"My laptop and your camera are in there. C'mon, just lock it."

He was unmoved.

We then muttered "so stubborn" at the same time. I got in the car and he climbed a stone wall.

Jason froze his nuts off looking at the West Bottoms. Longer than he or I wanted.

Finally he opened the car door, still sore.

"You ruined that."

"You ruined that. I'm not going to leave our shit in the car unlocked."

He pointed out that he was twenty feet from the car at all times. I pointed out that I was from New York.

LAYDEE

"What do you mean, the whole catastrophe?" my dad asked Willy.

Well, you gonna get married.
You gonna have kids.
You gonna buy a car.
Get a house in the suburbs,
And have a goddamn station wagon with four gallons of mayonnaise in the back.

Willy kept going on about the catastrophe that was about to befall my dad.

Minus the suburbs, he was right. Eve became my mom.

Willy had a Triumph. A green TR3 that he kept parked at a friend's garage. He couldn't leave it on the street. The car might get stolen, and, more than that, good luck finding a spot.

In New York City, parking your car is a blood sport. The sport was a little different during the 1960s. Meter maids hadn't taken steroids yet, and there was only one parking regulation sign on each block.

The sign on Morton Street originally read:

On Saturdays Willy took the TR3 out of the lot and parked it in front of his building. He would always give it a good wash. Sometimes he'd let a girl have a ride. Mostly he stood next to the car and looked cool.

Willy could park in front of his house because one day he climbed a ladder and painted over "SAT." on the parking sign with white enamel.

The car was another connection between Willy and my dad. Dad once had the same car, but his was baby blue, and he had abandoned it in Oklahoma.

After dropping out of college, before Morton Street, my dad drove his TR3 across the US. He would hit a big city, get a job, and stay till he felt like leaving.

When he reached Oklahoma City, my dad drove to the center of town to look around.

Near city hall his car starts getting pelted with buckshot. It wasn't someone shooting at him. The pellets were just falling from the sky. He drives around the other side of city hall and sees these guys with dogs scaring pigeons up to the sky. As soon as the pigeons get high enough, there is another crew that blows them away with shotguns.

The men shoot straight up so the bullets spit over the capitol dome and then land on the other side like hail.

In Oklahoma City, you could go to Woolworth's and buy guns over the counter next to peppermint sticks and sunflower seeds. If you weren't tall enough for the counter, they had kid-height bins full of squirrel guns.

So my dad bought a .380 Swiss automatic pistol.

He rented a room in a double-wide building downtown. Most of the other tenants were Native Americans. All the rooms had screen doors rather than regular doors. The building had long hallways with one bathroom per floor. There was a sink in each room and no air-conditioning.

It was summer and hot, hot, hot.

Cars didn't used to come with air conditioners. Dealerships and garages would install the ACs. Each car type was different and required a special mount. If you wanted an air conditioner you needed the right bracket. My dad got a job making those brackets.

He learned electro-welding, how to set up jigs, follow drawings, and not to duck under the drying brackets as hot paint dripped off them.

One day my dad is at work and in the office a guy is cleaning his gun.

"Hey, is that a .380?" my dad asks.
"Yeah," the guy answers.
"I have the same exact gun."
"Where?"
"Right here," says my dad, and he pulls the gun out of the back of his pants.
"Nice. It's a good one. How come you carry a gun?" asks the guy.
"How come *you* carry a gun?" asks my dad.
The guy pulls out a badge and says it is because he is a detective.
"Oh."
"That's how come I carry a gun, what about you?"
"I'm stupid," says my dad.
"Well, you shouldn't show it around," the detective says, and leaves it at that.

There was a gang of Oklahoma City guys my dad hung out with. Stupid guys with guns. The leader of them was named Bert. They would sneak into Tinker Air Force Base and go to drag races.

One night Bert borrowed my dad's TR3 and broke its axle. Another night Bert got in a fight with a little guy that bit his ear off.

A week later, after his ear had stopped bleeding, Bert decided they should all go find that little guy and kill him.

On hearing this, my dad decided it was time to go home, TR3 or not.

The .380 Swiss automatic came back with my dad to New York.

It was the gun that was in his ass crack when he told Raymond that Eve wasn't going back with him, ever.

My mom never went back to Raymond. She moved into my dad's apartment that night and they lived together for the rest of her life.

The apartment was at 38 Morton Street. An oblong sliver with a window that friends used as a drop box. My dad paid no rent, no gas, no electricity, and no telephone bill. He made fifty dollars a month.

But every week he had to clean up a flooded apartment.

Franny lived on the ground floor to the left of his door. She wore tinfoil hats, and the only place she was safe without one was in a completely full tub of water.

Two floors above Franny lived a Japanese woman with an elderly father. The woman was a nurse that worked the midnight shift and wore heels you could hear click-clack through the whole building.

When her father died she put him in a garbage bag and waited till Friday. That was the day you could put out big stuff like old mattresses.

Below her was a man that had screwed a piece of wood in the ceiling and rigged a mallet to a string. Every time the nurse got ready to go to work, slipping on her heels and click-clacking, the man below would pull the string over and over, banging the wood in competition.

Willy used to joke that my dad should get a lab coat and paint "attendant" on the back.

Franny's day job was to look through her peephole.

When my dad would come home she would shout in a voice that was a cross between an old bat, a toddler, and a strangled cat.

"Yeew fat yewish bastard," Franny would say anytime he entered or exited.

Every day.

"Yeew fat yewish bastard."
"Yeew fat yewish bastard."
"Yeew fat yewish bastard."
"Yeew fat yewish bastard."
"Yeew fat yewish bastard."

My dad went on a diet. He lost a hundred pounds. One day he comes home and he hears:

"Yeew yewish communist bastard."

He turned to the peephole, saw her eyeball, and said, "Well, thank you, Franny, you noticed."

When my mom moved in, Franny never said anything to her. But my mom, in a perfect copy of Franny's voice, would stand up for my dad:

"Yeew cwazy laydee. Lay in dee tub. Lay in dee tub. Cwazy laydee. Leeeeveee us olone. Geh awhey."

Eve

Through vigilance, luck, and help from Willy's camera equipment, my dad secured a golden ticket of an R.C. apartment for him and my mom at 54 Morton Street. It had the floor plan of a one bedroom, but was split between the basement and ground floor.

If you walked in the apartment there was immediately a balcony that overlooked the basement level. To the left was a sleeping area and the bathroom. To the right was a stairway down to the kitchen and living room. And if you looked up you would see a French bicycle hanging on two hooks.

My mom grew up in the Bronx. Her family was very poor. I think even poorer than Willy's. Her father was addicted to gambling.

He was also violent.

It sucked all around. But it sucked most to be my mom. She was treated like a slave and her parents never gave her anything.

But my mom's sister was given a bike. This made my mom not getting anything feel ten times worse.

There was no reason to it; I'm sure my mom was a good kid. She was so gentle.

As a school project, I was assigned to make my mother's family tree.

When I asked my mom for help she offered this: "Mara, you're creative, I give you permission to make it up. They won't know."

I made her parents from London, gave myself an aunt named Gumby, and drew a British flag.

I got an A, though I still don't know my grandfather's name.

The French bike that hung above in 54 was my mom's.

My father had helped her buy it.

Work was only a few blocks away, but my mom rode her bike there.

She rode the bike anywhere she could. It didn't matter where.

She loved that bike to an illogical degree.

But in the special logic of my family, she loved it just the right amount.

The wheel got stolen. Just the front one. My mom was a tough cookie, but she lost it. Cried day and night. To cheer her up and keep the bike safe, my dad used some spare window weights to hook up a pulley system in the apartment.

And my mom from then on loved hoisting her bike up every night to an illogical degree.

John's of Bleecker Street is famous for its brick oven and the fact that they don't sell pizza by the slice.

The slice thing wasn't a problem for my parents. A whole pie was the perfect amount for the two of them.

But John's didn't deliver.

The deal was, if my mom called in the order, my dad would pick it up.

My dad loves pizza. He loves all food, but pizza, Concord grapes, petit fours, and red Jell-O are the ones that get him emotional.

When my dad opens the box, he sees my mom has ordered anchovies on half of the pie. And somewhere between John's and 54 the anchovies have bled all over his side of the pizza.

The only foreign word besides *puta* my dad taught me was *anchovy*. *Anchovy* is Italian for shitty little fish.

When they went to bed, still angry, my dad tossed my mom's pillow over the balcony.

My mom had a thing about her pillows, and couldn't sleep without both pillows.

She was chewing gum, so she chewed it up faster and shoved it in his armpit.

A few years ago I found this note from my mom:

Kenny
I Love you!
Please dop being angry
at me. I promise Never
to put gum in your
arm pit again.

I Can't sleep without
you.
Eve.

I told my dad about the note. He is old now. It normally takes him a while to scan through his memories and find what I'm referring to.

So fast, in a maximum of three seconds, he said, "She wasn't sorry at all. She was bragging to everyone who came in The Store." Then he drifted off and missed her.

In the 1860s George Pullman invented luxury train travel. He manufactured sleeper cars with sheets and pillows. Dining cars with ornate restaurants and full kitchens. The cars were then rented rather than sold to the railroads, complete with servants. The servants were called porters. They made the berths into beds at night, helped with luggage, served food, shined shoes, and were on call twenty-four hours a day.

The porters were what put the "luxury" in luxury train travel. All Pullman porters were selected from a new windfall of low-paid workers: the blacks that had just been freed from slavery.

Pullman's cars were so successful that by 1920 his company was the largest employer of blacks in America.

Willy's father was a Pullman porter. Willy was one for a bit as well. It was steady pay, and the most respected job a black man could have at the time. Though it was working *kin to kant*, as Willy would say. From when you can see till you can't see.

The porters formed a union called the Brotherhood of Sleeping Car Porters (BSCP). It was founded by A. Philip Randolph.

This is Black History Month stuff. But they didn't teach me about it in my hippie public school where we called teachers by first names and learned about the Harlem Renaissance by memorizing poems:

Baby

Albert!
Hey, Albert!
Don't you play in dat road.
   You see dem trucks
   A-goin' by.
   One run ovah you
   An' you die.
Albert, don't you play in dat road.

                         —Langston Hughes

Willy taught me about the BSCP in the basement. This was part of the kiddo stuff.

The BSCP laid the tracks for the civil rights movement, with porters providing cash to the movement, and a knowledge that you could change things if you were unified. Also there was A. Philip Randolph, who went on to organize the first marches on Washington, and then the ones led by Martin Luther King, Jr.

Willy grew up *po*, but it didn't feel like it, because he grew up during the Great Depression.

If your father had any kind of steady pay during the Depression, you were bourgeoisie.

By default, having a job made you better off than 40% of the population.

There was a small deli case in The Store, filled with mostly mayo-based salads. Egg, tuna, chicken, potato, and so on. Every day my dad made a fresh roast beef and a few one-off items. The one-off items were always made with a customer in mind.

No matter what my dad stuffed—cabbage, peppers, mushrooms, veal, zucchini, rock Cornish hen—he knew Joseph Brodsky would buy one.

Brodsky would come in every night.

My father loved stuffing food, and Brodsky loved eating stuffed food. They had a perfect relationship.

"He was like a Russian heterosexual Oscar Wilde," my father says as the ultimate compliment.

Once Brodsky was asked what his favorite part of teaching at Columbia was.

"July and August," the poet replied.

When Brodsky wanted to quit smoking, he asked my dad to be the gatekeeper of his cigarettes, doling out two a day.

One night Brodsky came in, and my dad handed him a plastic donkey. Brodsky lifted the tail and a cigarette came out the donkey's asshole.

Our Store was more like an old general store than a grocery. When a customer came in, they didn't pull things off the shelf. My mom and dad would gather their order as customers listed the items they wanted. More often than not, my parents gathered the order before the customer had even crossed the street.

One day Willy came into The Store with a tape recorder. He pressed play, and a recording of his voice came on ordering a quart of milk.

My dad grabbed the milk from the fridge and put it on the pink counter.

Willy pressed play and a recording of him ordered a half pound of baloney. Then some beer. This went on till a small order was assembled.

Lots of other customers were in The Store watching this go down.

The tape recorder asks, *How much is that?*

My dad tells him the total.

You Jewish mother cocksucka. Us poor black people are here trying to live an . . . we ain't no Eskimos. We niggas! Willy is screaming, but it isn't Willy, it is a recording of his voice.

The order is bagged up and Willy pays for it.

Thank you, you fucking cocksucka, comes from the tape recorder.

Willy then walked out with his armful of groceries.

I think my dad had an orgasm. He took it as a gift. A gift that could only be given by someone who truly loved him.

ORDER OF THE UNIVERSE

"Was it a big deal to Willy, killing Cap'n Jack?" I ask my dad.

"Well, it wasn't, but it was because of the money, which eventually came back to haunt him. Without that money the landlord wouldn't have taken his senility and beaten him over the head with it, and taken power of attorney, and done all the other things. That eighty K from Cap'n was all the money Willy had. He never touched it."

"I was so pissed that she got Willy a funeral plot."
"That was probably one of the good things Garrison did!"
"I didn't know that."
"It was complicated."
"When I think back, it was like there was something wrong about Willy getting scammed. Like that was the wrong order of the universe."

"It was wrong, Garrison knew of his other ties. She did it behind their back, on the assumption that if nobody noticed Willy was senile, then fuck them all—they didn't care about him. And in fact, I didn't notice he was senile, because for me he was senile his whole fucking life. I thought it was funny that he would say he was going to Germany and come back the next day and I'd ask him how the sausage was. He did things like that all the time."

THE SMALL POND

As kids, my siblings and I played in traffic.

The game was: Run into the middle of the street, put down a water balloon, haul ass back to the sidewalk, and watch the oncoming cars run over the balloon. Repeat until you had a close call or ran out of balloons.

We also stayed up late, ate with our hands, cursed, never brushed our teeth, drank soda like it was water, and hung out at gay bars.

There was only one rule growing up: Don't touch the meat slicer.

The Store was a beautiful scrubby place with white enameled fridges and vintage cookie tins. But for me, nothing was as wonderful as the slicing machine. It was a streamlined silver sculpture manufactured by Hobart. Not the 410 designed by Egmont Arens. Our Hobart was a later model with a slanted meat feed. When the machine was turned on, it sounded like a circular saw, which is basically what it was. There was a carriage that most often held fresh roast beef. The carriage was pushed back and forth the way you rock a baby to sleep. Instead of peace and quiet, you got toilet paper–thin slices of meat.

No gory end. I have all my fingers. Loved the machine from afar until I hit 14, and the embargo was lifted. Then I loved it up close every day, eating translucent slices of turkey whether I was hungry or not.

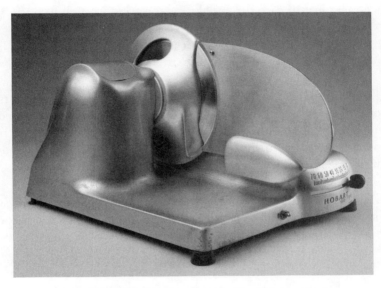

Hobart Model 410, 1940, designed by Egmont Arens

Before I was born, in the earliest days of The Store, if someone came in that gave my dad a bad feeling, he would camp out by the meat slicer.

The machine stood on rubber feet that acted like shock absorbers. They raised the slicing machine just enough so my dad's .380 Swiss automatic could live underneath. He would go pretend to slice meat just in case the spooky person tried to stick him up.

This was New York in 1972. It wasn't a question of will you be stuck up, it was a question of how often.

After a while my dad felt stupid. He got spooked by everyone and would hover behind the slicing machine like a coward. None of the people he got spooked by held him up. Even if they had, he wouldn't have drawn the gun. He could shoot cans in the woods, but not people.

So he ditched the gun for good and came up with a new tactic. If someone scary came in, he grabbed my mom, ran to the tailors across the street, and locked the door.

Gabe and Rita were the tailors across the street. They had Yiddish accents and smelled like mothballs. Rita taught me and my sister to sew by saying "in and out" over and over again.

The first time my dad fled to Gabe and Rita's with my mom was to get away from a spooky guy with brass knuckles on both hands. Mom and Dad watched from the safety of Gabe and Rita's as the spooky guy slunk around the counter to the register. The guy looked at them across the street and then he looked back at the register like it was booby-trapped, grabbed a six-pack of beer, and left.

From then on, if someone truly scary came in, my parents just fled across the street. It happened maybe two times a year till The Store turned into a restaurant. The restaurant was different from the grocery store. If a customer felt wrong, my dad just kicked them out, be they robbers or yuppies.

In hindsight, Dad's gun wouldn't have done any good. Almost every time my parents were stuck up it was some pleasant-looking person they never would have suspected.

Once, a guy who looked like he was going to buy a bag of chips pulled a gun and told everyone to get on the floor.

Our floor was covered in sawdust. The sawdust was delivered in sacks by a crippled Italian goombah from Queens. My dad had to unload the sacks from the back of the goombah's truck himself, but it didn't matter. He loved the sawdust. Every morning he and my mom sprinkled down the new floor. When I was little, Mom would give me a salad bowl of sawdust and I would help, dropping tiny pawfuls. If there was a spill, the sack of sawdust would come out and a thick wad of it would be laid down, turning the yellow shavings birch beer red or Coke brown.

At night all the sawdust was swept up. The floor sparkled because all the dirt from the day was absorbed by the sawdust. No mopping needed.

The health department said sawdust was not allowed, and just like that sawdust became a forbidden passion. And there are many passions that have since been forbidden by the DOH—cloth towels in the bathroom, fresh warm turkey, cooking with bare hands—but nothing hurt like the sawdust. I don't think my father has ever forgiven the City of New York.

I wasn't alive during this robbery, but my oldest brother, Charlie, was. He, my parents, and a few customers are facedown in sawdust. Charlie stands up and goes over to the guy with the gun who is raiding the register.

"Are you a hand robber?" Charlie asks the thief.
"Shut the fuck up," replies the thief.
"Charlie, get back here," my dad says. Charlie turns around and lies down in the sawdust.

The thief leaves.

Everything goes back to normal, minus some cash.

Later that same day Charlie is at a friend's. Tommy the taxi dispatcher and Jeff Goldblum the actor are in The Store. My dad is telling them about how Charlie mixed up "armed robber" with "hand robber."

A nice-dressed guy comes in and pulls out a .45.

There is almost no money in the register, because The Store was robbed in the morning. The guy is pissed and herds my mom, dad, Tommy, and Jeff Goldblum into the tiny bathroom in the back.

"Give me everything you got," the nice-dressed man says, waving his gun.

They all empty their pockets.

The thief takes fifteen dollars from my mom, forty off Tommy, twenty off my dad, and hands Jeff back his ten, saying, "You need this more than me."

My parents went out and ate lobster that night. If ever anything upsetting happened, we ignored it and went out to eat.

Pink and blue bathrooms at The Store

For a while we had a shopping routine at a strip mall in Paramus, New Jersey.

The strip mall had a supermarket next to a dark arcade filled with cabinet video games and pinball machines.

Mom would give us kids ten dollars each and we would disappear into the dark as our parents shopped for The Store and home.

My brothers played as many games as they could, running from game to game. Danny's favorite was 720°, a skateboarding game that always ended with your character getting attacked by killer bees.

All of me and Minda's quarters went to a game called Zookeeper, in which you had to build walls to keep animals from escaping.

Fifty dollars seems like a lot to drop in the 1980s, but it was a deal to keep us from asking to buy all kinds of crap in the supermarket, and the bonus of some quiet.

Also, the way my parents spent money defied gravity. They spent fifteen hundred dollars on an Apple IIC for Charlie when he was 9, because he asked for it.

Once we were coming back from playing Zookeeper and got in a car accident.

Fire trucks showed up fast, and the chief cut our battery wire so the car wouldn't explode.

It was noisy, flashing lights and all that.

As the car was being pushed out of the street, my dad said to my mom, "Are you hungry?"

We were in the Meatpacking District. At that time the only things in the neighborhood were people getting laid in empty meat trucks and Florent.

Florent was a restaurant, but people went to it for the waiters more than the food. They all acted like they were onstage, twirl-ing, shouting, and singing, performing a mix of spoken-word poetry, stand-up, and sashay.

The seven of us left the groceries to melt in the car and walked to Florent. We had a great time, ate some couscous and left the waiter a huge tip. By the end of it all I felt lucky we had gotten in a car crash.

The Store was open from 7:00 a.m. to 8:00 p.m. There weren't all-night grocery stores in the Village. But my mom and dad were close with their customers, so they gave them sets of keys. The customers could go in The Store any time of night. Take what they wanted and just write it down. Most of the customers had floating credit with us.

The city may have been more dangerous, but it was a less hostile place. Everyone knew each other. The rent stabilization laws were hard for landlords to beat, so people weren't forced to move out. They lived on the block forever. And that forever built a neighborhood.

Once, though, there was a crime wave.

Gabe and Rita kept getting robbed at night. They didn't keep any cash in the shop after the first time, so the thief stole silk shirts and pinking shears.

We got hit every week, too. The Store had a small window on Morton Street with an exhaust fan, and giant picture windows that looked out on Bedford Street.

Someone tiny kept crawling in the fan window at night, stealing cigarettes and cash. And when no cash was there they stole cigarettes and meat. Finally my dad put bars on the tiny window.

Next time the crook just shattered one of the picture windows. It cost three months' rent to replace, and in the end my dad wished he hadn't put the bars in.

In order to protect the big windows, my parents installed metal roll-down gates. It stopped the robberies, but the gates were so difficult and loud to raise that The Store had to stop being open twenty-four hours.

A woman named Nancy lived across Seventh Avenue by the taxi garage. She had a boyfriend my dad calls "Fagin."

He calls him Fagin because the guy ran a "school" out of Oliver Twist. Each week a van would unload a bunch of kids, and Fagin would tell them what places in the neighborhood to hit and how.

There was really nothing to do except for Gabe and Rita to get gates as well. Everyone on the block did, and the crime wave ended.

Our roll-down gates were like giant washboards that would make a kind of hillbilly music when they were pulled up and down. I couldn't open or close them till I was 15, but me and my sister always prepped the gates for my dad. We'd unlock the padlocks and pull the pegs—or the reverse at night, throwing them in a brass bucket that was full of dings and dents.

Willy never got stuck up. No one would pull that shit on him.

But he was robbed.

He won a competition in Missouri to play Crown in *Porgy and Bess* on Broadway.

He and Yvonne took the train to New York on one-way tickets, paid for by the producers of the opera. When he showed up to the theater they told him they were sorry, but his skin was too light to play Crown.

It wasn't news to him. He was always too light or too dark.

It never stopped him from going to auditions. He'd come in The Store singing, practicing, serenading.

My mom would sing to wake us up for school.

♫ "Rise and shine! And give God your glory, glory! Rise and shine!" ♪

But the way my mom sung it was awful. We would all cover our ears and leap out of bed. Her song was a threat, like: if you don't wake up, I am shipping you kids to a Christian cult in Waco.

If Willy had sung it, we would have woken up and sat mesmerized.

The thought of Willy singing "God's glory glory" makes me cry.

In the cabaret circuit Willy was a big fish. The whole club would hush when he sang. He did a trick where he'd hold a note forever. The note would be pure and echo off the walls, adding to itself over and over again.

But he wasn't happy to be in the small pond, and was always searching for a big break.

All my dad wanted was to stay in his small pond.

There were two businesses on Morton Street. Both were grocery stores. That's how and why my dad decided to run a grocery.

The owners asked the same price to buy their businesses, even though one store was twice the size of the other. The larger one had newer fridges and more inventory. The smaller one was half a block closer to Willy's stoop.

My dad chose the smaller one.

My parents wore aprons and wrapped cold cuts in wax paper. They sold Wonder Bread, and mayonnaise. They rotated the milk and butter, putting the newest stock in the back.

An old cash register would ring every time a sale was made. It seemed like a regular store.

But it really wasn't.

My parents were freethinkers, keyed into gonzo journalism and drugs.

The grocery store they ran was a wonderful, fucked-up cartoon version of a general store. Even Mr. Magoo could see it; there were a hundred and two clues.

Prime retail space was taken up by a big rocking chair that was often filled with Willy.

Whatever my dad put near the door got shoplifted. So he created a community bookshelf. Take a book leave a book, or just take a book.

On Wednesdays my parents gave away plastic dinosaurs to kids. You didn't need to buy anything, really, you just needed to walk by and be under 12.

Everybody seemed to know each other's name, and if they didn't, my mom or dad introduced them.

The biggest clue was the feeling of the place. It wafted at you that my mom and dad loved stocking cans on the shelves. And it was cool if you just wanted to buy some Brillo pads or Ivory Snow, but that wasn't all you were supposed to get out of the exchange.

Also, there were the antique gumball machines that took up half the counter. They all worked and cost a penny each. If one jammed, the world stopped, and my dad wouldn't slice baloney till it was fixed.

It started small. A red Pulver machine found at a flea market—the wall-mounted type that used to be found in every subway station. The machine had a smiling cop made of pressed tin holding a sign. When you put your penny in, the sign turned from "stop" to "go," and a piece of wrapped gum dropped down.

It was just that one machine for a while, not such a big clue.

But then my dad found Billy the Baker Boy. He found him at a junk store in New Jersey.

The machine looked like a kid's drawing of a house, with a roof made of gumballs, and a big window that revealed a chef whose hand was permanently attached to an oven door.

After you put your penny in and turned the lever, Billy would open the oven, scoop out a gumball, drop it into a trough that was connected to a pipe; then the gumball would drop out of the pipe into your hand.

The machine was special. It wasn't an ironic interpretation of life. It was life. Billy was at work, he had a job. His job was, when you put the penny in, he had to get you a gumball. It wasn't make-believe like the cop machine; Billy really did his job and you got a gumball as proof.

And with that my dad was hooked. Everywhere he went he looked for gumball machines.

He subscribed to a monthly magazine called *Antique Trader*. The magazine was, at its heart, classified ads. He would scan the coin-operated section like a junkie.

"What is wrong with those assholes looking for frogs and ceramic owls? I can't believe those jerks wasting their time when there are all these great gumball machines."

Pikes Peak was a trapezoid-shaped machine. You had to get a metal ball to defy gravity by turning one knob back and forth just so. It didn't give gum. If you won you just got your penny back.

There was a nickel machine. It held chocolate-covered peanuts in a big glass dome. When you turned the knob it would play "Pop Goes the Weasel," and it wouldn't give you your peanuts till the end of the song. The last note of the song was the sound of peanuts hitting the trapdoor. The song was so long that when the peanuts finally came it was a shock, like a jack-in-the-box.

My dad had to start rotating the machines, because there wasn't enough room. Nights were spent winding and greasing the clock-works.

Not only were the machines mostly a penny, but if a customer asked "Do the machines work?" my dad just handed them twenty pennies.

He didn't care that the machines were worth money, that they were antiques and sometimes one of a kind. The machines were there to be played. He loved them and took care of them like they were his children. Sharing their small pleasures, movements, and minor victories with whoever walked in.

PLEASE !
Do <u>NOT</u> Hit or
SHAKE THE GUM
MACHINES.

"Get the fuck off my machine. Get the fuck out," my dad would shout.

That was if you were lucky.

One little girl was particularly rough with a machine. My dad told her parents, "If she hits my machine like that one more time, I'm gonna hit her just the same way."

The girl and her family never came in again.

As soon as my dad started having kids he stopped buying gumball machines.

The machines were still in The Store, but the collection started to shrink rather than grow.

I remember my dad selling them when we needed money, like a rainy day fund—if my brother needed a root canal or a compressor broke. But my dad says he just sold them because after we were born, he all the sudden didn't give two shits about them.

Eventually the gumball machines were sent to the basement, and replaced with some new clue that The Store wasn't a regular store.

Yvonne was a hole you threw money into.

Even though she was pretty much married to another guy named Louie, Willy and her never divorced. They were separated for sure, but they didn't sever ties till she died.

Dad would tell Willy stories about the butcher, and Willy would tell my dad about Yvonne.

She was always trying to get Willy to do something risky, dangerous, stupid, or evil, but he never stopped talking to her.

Yvonne and Louie lived in Harlem. Louie ran a travel agency that catered specifically to black people. It was one of the first agencies to do that, so he did really well.

Louie was pussy-whipped, and the money just went straight into the Yvonne pit.

Willy would go up there a lot. I don't know what he did. But I know Yvonne gambled, did coke and amoral acts, because that is all Willy wanted to talk about with my dad when he got back to the Village.

Yvonne died playing poker. Collapsed on a card table, face full of chips. She overdosed and had a heart attack in the middle of a hand.

"I guess she died happy," was my dad's response to the news.

What a stupid fucking bitch doing coke with a heart condition, Willy replied.

But my dad knew he was shattered about it.

Coke and amoral acts may just have been what my dad liked to hear about. And maybe that's why Willy didn't talk about the other stuff.

The other stuff was likely music.

Willy was wrapped up in it all his life. My dad had no interest.

When they talked about Willy playing Arthur's Tavern, they talked about his regular gig in winter as a spotter.

Customers would come to the club wearing big, heavy coats. There was no coat check; this was the Village. Everyone hung their coats on a row of hooks at the back of the room.

Willy would sing a set, but he also hung out all night.

Even onstage he was watching the room, trying to spot a type—a man or woman that came in wearing no coat.

After he spotted one, he'd track them till they left, making sure they didn't leave with someone else's coat.

The stories Willy told my dad about singing at the Five Spot were mostly about how the bartenders stole. You could be standing right next to them and have no idea. The stories always ended with a universal truth: there is nothing anyone can do to stop a bartender from stealing.

They talked about anything but music.

And I wonder if Willy's pond really was so small.

The Arvell that Willy hit with a pipe as a kid was Arvell Shaw, Louie Armstrong's bassist. A lot of the boys that beat up Willy went on to become famous musicians. St. Louis at that time was crawling with talent and clubs. Willy became a figure in the scene.

When he met Yvonne they became the heart of a musicians' clique.

I can't imagine anyone cooler than Willy.

He must have seemed like he was from space with his red hair and freak voice. A voice that sounded like Paul Robeson's, only softer. But just as powerful and sad.

Then add to him the uninhibited Yvonne, who was nut-sack-busting gorgeous. There is a photo of her I remember. She wore pearls, a low-neck blouse, and Egyptian-style eyeliner. She was mixed race with smooth skin that was darker than Willy's.

They were hot shit.

And this didn't change when they got to New York. They fell into the same type of circle, but even more talented and hip. The "we ain't no Eskimos" Charlie from building 40 was Charlie "Bird" Parker.

I know nothing about jazz, but I know who Charlie Parker is. He is the top floor.

THE TOP FLOOR

"That's nothing, tell Jason he's a pussy," Zack says, and turns his arms over at me. Burns and scars line them. The scars are exactly like mine, except he has more. Milky Way–shaped marks that are concentrated below the wrists.

"It's out of hand. You need to talk to your dad. You need to figure something out," Jason told me last night, the fourth thing he said after three weeks away. "You should wear a long-sleeve shirt" was the fifth.

Zack stops cooking for a second, turns, and says, "When you get home just tell Jason . . . this is a fucking kitchen."

That is what I told Jason last night, followed by: A long-sleeve shirt standing in front of a 350-degree slab of steel? I'd rather get burned.

I don't notice them.

The marks have been on my arms for half my life. Longer than I've been with Jason.

He notices them every so often. Not in a sweet concern for my well-being, more in "be careful, you stupid idiot."

Zack calls out to my dad and says, "Jason is being a pussy."

My dad answers that Jason has the right to be a pussy, equal society, modern era, etc., and asks Zack if he stirred the chili.

At 10:00 a.m., the doors to the market are unlocked. Customers file in. The weekend regulars are already seated. They have snuck in through the maintenance door. Some of them got here before me. Half of them were here yesterday when we opened at nine.

The Store has been in the Lower East Side for ten years. Credit should forever go to my sister for finding it a new home planet.

The Store is not the same, but neither is New York. Neither are we. My father is 74. Some days he is on. It is difficult to keep up, and everything he cooks is light-years beyond my ability. Other days he sits in his chair talking to customers and gets up to cook only when he has to.

And when he has to, it is a shit show.

Not the food. My father is the shit show.

Physically turning from the cutting board to the griddle is a challenge. He'll forget ingredients—title ingredients, like the cashews in Patsy's Cashew Chicken.

If I reach behind him to get bread, he will explode because I've broken his concentration and now he can't remember what he's put in the dish.

Worse than the explosion is the whimper.

The shit show whimper is the sound of my dad holding back tears, praying that the Ten Condiments sandwich will not topple over. It is a sound that could make stones cry.

The safest, kindest thing to do is stand off to the side and not cook—be there if he needs anything. This is what Zack does. But Zack has a gift for being chill.

I have no such gift. It is a special kind of torture for me.

When the rhythm is good, and my father doesn't have to pee, the three of us cooking together is the best. I live for it. I'd die for it. I arrange my life around it.

Luke, the waiter, pokes his head in the kitchen and says, "Some asshole wants the eggs scrambled on their Blisters. I wouldn't ask, but you always do it for Michelle."

"It's fine. I'll do it," Zack says.

I put down three corn tortillas for the Blisters and turn up the left side of the griddle because "BPFT—B" is also on the check.

"BPFT—B" is Banana Pecan Brown Sugar Bread Pudding French Toast.

"Be on guard. I really fucked with the menu," my father shouts from his chair at the center of the dining area. This is my father's mantra.

I crack three eggs in a bowl and add some cream and vanilla.

"If you get kids' pancakes, I need to get up," my dad adds.

"You don't want to know," Zack says to me, making scrambled eggs.

Zack has become the captain of The Store. He is the rock that cleans the grease trap and broils the brisket.

I am not a rock. I am a tiny pebble that likes to cook very fast and only on weekends.

A buzzer goes off.

Cubed ciabatta soaked in French toast batter blankets the front of the griddle. I embed it with bananas, pecans, and sprinkle brown sugar on top.

The buzzer is still buzzing.

I flip the BPFT—B over with a giant spatula.

To the right of the griddle is the steam table. It is where we keep stocks (veggie, chicken, beef) and a few base ingredients like marinara sauce or chili that my dad and Zack cook each morning. The flame needs to be turned on and off every half hour so the bases don't burn or fall below temperature.

I turn the steam table off and reset the timer for another half hour.

The buzzing stops.

Zack is going to an amusement park with his girlfriend tomorrow. She has never been. He is thinking of buying them a special ticket that lets you bypass all the lines, but there are different levels and he can't decide if he should get the "Executive" or the "VIP."

I ladle black beans and ranchero from the steam table into a metal bowl with spinach, rice, and sliced jalapeño. This slurry is for the inside of Zack's Blisters.

Zack takes the tortillas off the griddle and lines a sizzle tray with them, pours the rice slurry down, tops it with the scrambles and some cheddar cheese. Then puts the whole thing into the broiler till it blisters. The dish is normally made with sunny eggs, and the trick is to make sure the yolks don't get hard.

I flip my BPFT—B over. The brown sugar has melted into trophy polish for the bits of pecans and chunks of bread.

"Nice," Zack says, ringing the bell for Luke to pick up his Blisters.

Zack has gotten a lot of sleep. I can tell this because he will not shut up. It is sweet how excited he is for Jasmine to have her mind blown by the Kingda Ka. I totally agree. She is gorgeous; he is a lucky guy. Wow: two years you guys have been together. Yeah, I'd love for her to be in the family.

I drip molten brown sugar on the underside of my wrist. Zack asks if I need the burn cream, with an inflection of, "Are you a pussy?" I am not.

"Luke, this goes to the same place," I say, and push my BPFT—B through the pickup window.

My brother drinking till 3:00 a.m. the night before work sounds irresponsible and depressing, but when it actually happens it is great. He is less cocky and doesn't have the energy to tell me facts about the Mets and baby animals.

"I got huevos," my brother says. There are lots of items on the check, but only two are up for debate. The other is a country scramble with blue cheese. "Okay, I got the CS7. You got bacon and English muff," I say, and put down an order of pancakes. It makes more sense for me to take the huevos, but: (1) His huevos are better than mine, and (2) He HATES blue cheese.

Zack doesn't like to talk about my dad dying, but he has told me that blue cheese will be off the menu before the body is cold.

It is 10:10 and someone just ordered "Soup A" for breakfast.

"Dad, you're gonna have to get up," Zack shouts.
"Now? What is it?" my dad answers.
"No, one check away, African Green Curry."
"You can come in now," I shout, and flip my pancakes.
"Let's just finish this check first," Zack says, lifting the lid to his huevos. I give him marinara, beans, collards, and chicken stock.

My dad comes in the kitchen. I shoot Zack a sorry face, because he was right about finishing the check. But I'm not sorry; my dad got up fast. That is a good sign.

"Bok choy, broccoli, snow peas, cabbage," my dad says, taking my spot in front of the griddle.

Zack calls to the dishwasher for bok choy and broccoli from the walk-in. I reach behind my dad and plate my pancakes. Zack shakes his head.

My father heats up a pan with olive oil. "Using the griddle, okay?" I say, and throw down corn tortillas.

I put the last one down right as my dad turns to scoop his chopped onions, cabbage, bok choy, and any other green vegetables we have on hand in the pan.

Zack flips my country scramble eggs and I add the blue cheese. The dishwasher gives me a tortilla holder that I fill and put in the pickup window. Zack rings the bell as he plates his huevos.

"Did you do the bacon?" I ask Zack, and send the CS7.

"Thai curry," my dad says, adding a big ladle of veggie stock to the browned vegetables. Zack dips down in the fridge, and hands him a jar.

I squirt pancakes on the griddle and ask Zack to make fried chicken.

My dad hands me a whisk and says, "Mix in the curry and peanut butter really good. Am I done?"

Zack scans the checks and says, "Yeah, you can sit down."

"Did you hear? Jasmine has never been to an amusement park. There are major upsides to growing up on an island," my dad says, tucking his rag into his apron.

Me and Zack clear a path. The space we cook is narrower than the aisle of a bus.

"I want pictures. I want it of her face on the first ride. You can send the soup. Maybe put some spinach in the bowl," my dad says, and heads for his chair.

It is a light-years day. The soup is my sister's favorite thing on the menu. A menu that is thirty-five years long.

The buzzer rings. We have more to go, but it is late enough to just leave the steam table off. "Good day. Good checks," Zack says.

He says this at the exact steam table moment every weekend.

He says it even if we have gotten in a screaming fight. If my dad has been belligerent and ornery, if I sat down on the floor and sobbed till my apron was soaking wet, if all the dishes went to the wrong tables, if the fridge broke, if he overcooked the brisket and the turkey.

My brother loves The Store. The good and the bad.

No matter what has happened, no matter if he insulted my dishes and secretly hoped my gravy would clump. No matter if he didn't do my side of bacon. At the steam table point, when he says "Good day," I love my brother.

My dad is in his chair talking to a woman he tried hard to kick out for bringing an outside coffee in. She threw it away and apologized. He has been talking to her for half an hour.

"Dad, I have kids' chocolate chip pancakes," I shout from the kitchen.

He doesn't want to get up, and tells me that I need to make three baseball-size pancakes and then put a stick in each.

My dad warns that it might not work, he has not tried it yet.

Zack shakes his head.

I can't find the sticks.

"So fucking stupid," Zack says as he finds the sticks for me. The bag is unopened.

One time, Zack stopped talking. Not just hangover-level volume, which still has a few comments and baseball facts. This was mute. The only exchange unrelated to cooking was when he thought my dad had called for him, but then it turned out my dad had just said, "Exactly."

"*I fucking hate that word!*" Zack screamed.

Be careful what you wish for. I cooked for as long as I could stand.

"Zack, are you mad at me?" I asked.
"No," Zack said.
"Did Dad lay into you bad this morning?"
"No."
"What the F is going on?"
"Nothing, let's just cook."
"Really?"

"Let's just cook"? This is not what Zack believes in. I think I said, "Really, c'mon," twenty times till he finally broke. "My kickball team captain was screwing another team's captain. They stopped fucking and now neither will play. It is so fucked up."

It took me a while to understand. There were rules about the number of girls per team. I don't really understand still. But I understood that the kitchen without Zack was no fun. I told him, and just like that, the day turned. The items broke even between griddle and stove. Now and then my dad would pop in and join the line.

And when the steam table moment hit, Zack said, "Great cook, good checks," and we bumped knuckles.

"We were wrong," I say to Zack as I plate the kids' pancakes and ring the bell.

They get a "Whoa" from Luke.

"How did they come out?" my father asks.

Zack pops out of the kitchen to check on the item.

He reports back: the kid is eating the pancakes just like a lollipop. Our dad is a genius.

BUCKETS OF GRAVY

The first time John Belushi came in to The Store, he ordered an egg sandwich.

John looked at the sandwich, raised his eyebrows, and took a huge bite, filling his cheeks like a chipmunk.

He went through every sort of emotion you could have while chewing. Then he spit the huge bite on the counter. "That's fucking terrible," he said, smiled, and watched my mom and dad fall in love with him.

He had a key to The Store just like half the block. Sometimes my dad would open in the morning and find John asleep in the rocking chair, a pack of Bounty towels acting as a pillow.

Famous at this point, John tried to take people from his regular life to help them out or just to have them around. He asked my dad to cater the set for his movie *Neighbors* that was filming on Staten Island.

My dad would wake up at 5:30 a.m., slicing cold cuts and making salads, but mostly he made melon balls. That was what they wanted. Honeydew, cantaloupe, watermelon, all placed in separate containers. He made gallons of them, and quickly became an expert, cutting the melons just so, ensuring there were no seeds in any balls.

Why did they want melon balls? My dad says they were all on coke. He says this like it is a simple equation. Two plus two equals four—cocaine plus Staten Island equals melon balls.

John told him to charge as much as his imagination could create for the catering, and then double it.

At the end of the first week, my dad got a check for $1,500. The raw materials (aka melons) couldn't have cost more than a hundred dollars. My father had never made that much profit in his life. He was excited, and bragged about it to Bobby the Teamster.

Bobby the Teamster was John's driver. Bobby's father was a teamster chauffeur too. His brothers and uncles were all drivers as well. It was some sweet deal, but Bobby was a nice enough guy.

"You know that's what I make every week, and all I do is sit in the limo and get stoned," Bobby said. Which was true. He drove John to the set, and would then just do cocaine and eat melon balls for the rest of the day.

At first my dad felt like a sucker, but came to the realization that keeping score with money was meaningless. He had a lot more fun learning how to get balls with no seeds than Bobby had sitting on his ass in another planet.

On the first day of shooting *Neighbors*, the lead actress's husband said he wouldn't let her leave the hotel until he got $14,000 in cash.

John set up a time to drop off the money.

A man named Bill Superfoot was guarding John at the time. Not against other people, but against himself.

In the mornings when my dad would find John sleeping at The Store, it was bittersweet.

Sweet: John looked cute fast asleep hugging a pack of paper towels to his face.

Bitter: John was there because his wife, Judy, had locked him out of the apartment. And Judy had locked him out because John was using drugs.

When the time came to drop the $14,000 in cash, John went up to the hotel room with Superfoot.

They didn't bring any money.

Superfoot "had a talk" with the husband. The actress went to the set. She was wonderful, the movie started on time.

The Armenian who sold The Store to my dad had run the place for sixty years.

Along with the inventory, equipment, and lease, my dad got two days of training.

One of the things the Armenian taught my dad was to add a tiny touch of salt to the coffee before you grind it.

Why? It didn't matter. My dad added a tiny touch of salt every time he ground the coffee.

My parents hired a sweet delinquent named Dominic to be a delivery boy and store clerk. They taught him to do the daily tasks like breaking down boxes and grinding coffee.

One day a customer complains that the coffee tastes strange.

The next day my dad watches Dominic dump the coffee beans into the grinder, carefully check the grind knob, and slowly sprinkle way too much salt in. Dominic starts to close the lid, and reach for the "on" switch.

"Wait!" my dad shouts.

Dominic freezes. My dad grabs a spoon and opens the lid. He goes to scoop out the extra salt, looks down, and sees that Dominic has drawn a perfect "D" out of the salt.

My dad always eschewed publicity. By "eschewed," I mean actively fought against it and blacklisted anyone who wrote about The Store.

When The Store became a restaurant, it became famous for not wanting to be reviewed or talked about. People would call, and my dad would say, "Sorry, Shopsin's is out of business. New York City rent, ya know." If they asked my dad, "Where are you located?" he would answer, "Next to the phone," and hang up.

Every commercial business in NYC had to take care of the garbage they made. Some owners hired a private company to pick the trash up weekly or daily, keeping the bags in their basement, putting them out at night. Other owners put the bags in the trunks of their cars and drove them home to Queens.

We had a dumpster. It was forest green and pressed against the wall around the corner from The Store. A company would come pick it up once a week.

Our dumpster was in a sad state. It had been dropped so many times. Wheels had been broken off. The lid was bent. One day the garbage company replaced the dumpster. It was a gift from the gods. My dad was excited. The dumpster wasn't refurbished or repainted; it was brand-new and brought him pure joy.

Later that same day a sanitation inspector comes into The Store. "I'm giving you a violation," the inspector says. "The lid to your container is open," he continues.

"Show me," my dad says.

They go outside, and the sparkling clean dumpster lid is open. The dumpster is empty except for one small clear bag of garbage.

"It's not my garbage. I didn't leave the lid open," my dad says.

My dad is right. It is not restaurant garbage, no way, no how. Goldilocks has left us her apartment's trash and didn't even bother to close the lid.

This is the drawback of a dumpster. Your basement doesn't stink, you don't need to put the bags out, but people think the dumpster is free like air. It isn't—we had to pay by the pound.

The inspector said he was giving us a ticket anyway. My dad asked to speak to his supervisor, to which the inspector said the supervisor was not available.

It got very quiet. My dad went inside The Store. He came out with a huge handful of flour and threw it in the inspector's face.

POLICE LINE DO NOT CROSS

Six cops showed up, guns drawn.

The sanitation inspector had called it in as an assault.

One of the cops was happy when he figured out what had happened. He had a sister who owned a hardware store. Next to her store was a little vegetable grocery, and the sister was going nuts from all the sanitation tickets for orange rinds and banana peels left in front of her part of the sidewalk.

The sanitation inspector is still covered in flour. A few guns are still drawn, though the cops seem to be on my dad's side.

The writer Calvin Trillin shows up to get lunch, and without a skip asks my mom, "What's the charge, assault with intent to bake?"

The case was settled with a "consent decree." All my dad had to do was agree never to throw flour at a sanitation inspector again.

The lawyer that won the case was a beautiful woman named Valerie. She represented my dad for free.

Valerie was a regular in The Store. The regulars were always giving us things. Free meals at restaurants they ran, Rolling Stones concert tickets for my mom, computer programs for my brother, dental work, theater tickets, T-shirts, shoes, a tour of a television studio, a laser printer—the list goes on forever. I call them regulars, but they were more than customers.

Sometimes we would barter. A trip to St. Barts was paid for with a year's worth of Burmese hummus and shrimp gumbo.

My dad had a standing deal with Calvin (Bud) Trillin. Publishers were always sending Bud cookbooks to review. Now and then Bud would bring big stacks of the books to The Store in exchange for food credit.

My dad would pore over the cookbooks, putting his own version of a recipe on the menu. He would get a Greek cookbook from Bud, and the next week, as soon as he figured out where to get the best feta, the menu would double in size.

The Store's kitchen wasn't in a separate room. All that stood between my dad and the dining room was a stainless steel shelf and a specials board. The shelf was propped up with cans of black beans that no longer had labels. The specials board was written in every color of dry erase marker that my dad could find. This was only six colors, but it looked like more.

Pendant lamps hung from a pressed tin ceiling. Plastic dinosaurs were used as ketchup bottle caps. Good luck dollar bills were taped to the walls. The smell of burning butter or roasting brisket was constant.

Also constant were me and my siblings crawling in between customers' legs as they ate. We learned it was okay from our mom, who whenever it came time to take an order would pull up a chair or scootch into a customer's booth. No matter if it was the first time the customer was in our place or the hundredth.

Every dish that left the kitchen was put on the stainless steel shelf. There were no heat lamps. My mom had to drop whatever she was doing and pick up the food before it got cold. If she didn't, my dad would scream and shout.

My parents fought like crazy. Gum in the armpit was the least of it. Fighting was like breathing to my parents.

"Stupid, no-good cunt," my father would scream from the kitchen.

"How 'bout some bread and butter with your soup?" my mom would ask a customer, as if nothing was wrong.

"That's it. I've had it," my dad would mutter, almost crying.

Finally my dad would push a plate onto the shelf and shout, "Pickup!" My mom would rush to get it, and the fight would be over.

The Store as a restaurant

For a while we were listed in New York guidebooks as a shoe store. It was my dad's idea, but it was easy to get customers in on the game of hiding us from *Zagat's* and *Fodor's*.

It was clear why people tried to find us. My dad cooked hundreds of soups to order from a tiny kitchen. On top of that, there was the celebrities.

Packs of them. Movies were shot in California but cast in New York. Directors, writers, actors, producers, each name bigger than the next, would tip each other off on this great shithole in the Village run by a militant Buddha and his wife.

JFK Jr. was a regular. He would glide in on Rollerblades.

This was a gift from my father to my mother. Most businesses had signs that prohibited dogs, skateboards, and roller skates. My dad was all for such rules. Any other customer would have been kicked out fast for wearing Rollerblades to lunch.

But not JFK Jr.

Because if JFK Jr. was wearing Rollerblades it meant he would be wearing Lycra bike shorts.

And my mother thought he was the sexiest man alive. It was a self-sacrificing kindness by my father, who would argue that the sexiest man or woman ever to come in the restaurant was the father of the model Cindy Crawford.

Maybe it was the actors that led to the models. We always had salad on the menu, but no one would say our food was light. They came in droves, sweet and freakishly pretty, bumping their heads on the lights. Tomato Cream with Garlic Croutons was the soup they all got. It was a tomato soup made to order using marinara sauce as a base with a touch of heavy cream and a ladle of veggie stock. Half a baguette was spread with garlic, butter, and cheddar, then put under the broiler till it bubbled. The broiled bread was chopped and sprinkled into the soup.

The models brought in more models and their boyfriends— magicians, rock stars, nightclub owners, and athletes.

The rock stars brought in rock stars. The magicians brought in comedians and cult icons. And it went on in this circle. We had circles of customers who were printers, and motion graphic specialists. There were circles of young people on their way, directors, brain surgeons, the first website designers. But the celebrities were the easiest circle to spot.

At night my mom would work the counter and the cash register, while a gum-chewing waitress with red hair named Kate worked the tables.

Once there was a two-top that placed its order with Kate. One customer got a cup of chicken soup, and the other a bowl of split pea. Kate put the order on the spindle and spun it toward my dad. As Kate turned around, the two-top signaled her. "Can you change the chicken soup to split pea?" the customers asked.

"My pleasure," said Kate. She turned toward the kitchen and screamed, "Hold the chicken and make it pee."

A side of baguette with butter was "grease me up a big one." With no butter was "leave it alone."

"Leave now you'll be early" was my dad's response to customers that said they were in a hurry. It was Store policy and Kate said it at least once a night.

One night Kate didn't like a table of four from the get-go; they were in a rush. "Ha ha . . . ha," the table said when Kate explained that they could be early if they left now.

The four put in an order getting this, this, and that. A woman at the table wearing a blue headband was ruder than the rest.

The Store was not an easy place to work. There was only one waitress, no busboys, and thirty seats. It was like playing pinball, but you were the ball instead of the flippers.

It began to fill up and Kate started to bounce.

She brought the four-top sodas and went to start another table.

Pickup. Salads, butter-broiled breads, a cheddar corn chowder, and more were brought to the four-top.

Kate had ten tables going. Blue headband flagged her down and shoved the corn chowder at Kate, saying it had bacon.

"So what?" asked Kate. The woman said she couldn't eat bacon.

Kate brought the soup back to my dad in the kitchen. This happened not a lot, but enough. Sometimes my dad fucked up; he would taste the returned dish and if it was wrong, he would drop everything to make it right.

But that is not what he did here.

"ALL CHOWDER HAS BACON IN IT," my dad said, buried in checks.

The chowder was not ladled from a big vat. Onions, carrots, celery, baked potato, and bacon were sautéed in a pan till soft. Flour and sherry were added to thicken, next came chicken stock, lots of corn, cheddar, and a squirt of cream.

Kate brought the soup back to blue headband and explained that all chowder has bacon in it, that my dad was not going to remake the soup, and asked the woman if she could swap dishes with someone else at the table.

The woman asked why we were being such hard-asses.

Kate went back to my dad.

"Kick them the fuck out," said my dad.

Kate went back to the table of four.

"You guys are really dicks," said blue headband.

The others at the table were still digging into their food. They took headband's side, though not actively.

Kate began to bus the table.

She took their plates away in mid-bite. Everything went in the bus tray, the chowder, the sodas, and bread. Before Kate could grab the big Caesar salad, blue headband picked it up. The woman then poured the salad over the booth seat behind her, and called Kate a "fucking bitch."

Kate took a Coke from the bus tray, poured it over the woman's head, and called her the same.

"I want to see the manager," the woman screamed.

My dad walked out from the kitchen and explained that he thought it best if the four left. And then he walked straight back to cook his checks.

The four left with the headband woman shouting, "Fuck you."

As they were out the door, Kate whipped around and asked, "Anybody else?"

The whole restaurant, my parents included, exploded in applause and the bag of sawdust was brought out.

A man who drove a cute little blue Jetta lived across the street from The Store in Gabe and Rita's building. At the time my dad drove a motorcycle, and was always competing with this guy for the legal parking spot nearest to The Store.

The man came into The Store one morning and asked for half a baguette to go. My mom charged him for the half a baguette.

Then he said he would like the bread buttered.

My mom tried to charge him fifty cents extra. The man was upset that he had to pay for butter in a "place like this."

"This" brought my dad to the front of The Store. He argued that we had to buy the bread, cut and butter it, and throw away the stale baguettes every night. Then we had to wrap it all up and put up with lousy jerks.

The man left The Store without his half a baguette.

Our baguettes were perfect, with crispy crusts. The stales were used for fencing. Victory was yours if the enemy's sword folded in half. Sometimes we wouldn't throw the bag of stales out. We'd leave them in a corner for three days. The super-stale sword hurt more, but when you won, your opponent's sword would burst into bread crumbs.

Some days no one ordered pumpernickel. But we always had it fresh because it was my mom's favorite bread. If it wasn't ordered for two straight days, I would make Frankenstein shoes out of the untouched loaves, and clomp around in the sawdust.

The cute-Jetta man came into The Store only one other time. It was late in the day, and it was to ask what had happened to his car.

Early that morning my dad was setting up The Store. All the gates were down. It was around 5:00 a.m.

My dad heard our dumpster being picked up. Then he heard a loud bang. He rolled up the gate and saw the garbage truck had bonked the lamppost. The post had come crashing down onto the cute blue Jetta.

Crazy Frankie from across the street took a Polaroid of the scene and gave it to my dad. The garbage truck driver scratching his head; the lamppost still working somehow.

The city came and righted the lamppost. You would never have known what happened, except for some shrapnel and an abstract sculpture of a blue Jetta.

When the man who didn't want to pay fifty cents for butter asked my dad if he knew what happened to his car, in a rare moment of self-control, my father didn't say a word.

Food at The Store was all over the map. Turkey sandwiches next to Bok Choy Bop. African Green Curry, Indonesian grilled chicken, huevos rancheros, matzoh ball soup all in the same column.

Everything was delicious. Except when it wasn't. My father wasn't afraid of failure. The dishes weren't tested over and over. Sometimes he would make it once for my mom. Mostly, he'd put items on the menu he had never made before. The dishes would get better each time he made them, or they would be taken off.

My mom had great taste buds. "Add lemon," she'd say. Too much salt, it was better before, more cheese, less garlic, make it crisper, add some avocado.

Cheeseburger Soup: a hamburger made on the griddle, placed on a toasted bun, then the whole thing put in a bowl with a made-to-order cheddar chowder poured over it.

The way my dad cooked was not authentic to the dish, but it was authentic to my dad.

Charlotte Zwerin was a favorite customer of my mom and dad.

A talented director and editor, she worked with the Maysles brothers on their early documentaries *Salesman* and *Gimme Shelter*. She didn't just work for them; she was a partner and one of the reasons their movies were great.

"She was just specially wonderful. There were certain people that would come in, and there is a sense of serenity that comes in with them," is how my dad describes Charlotte.

Percy Spencer invented the microwave oven. He was working at a place called Raytheon in 1945, on radar equipment for the Allied forces.

Percy was experimenting with magnetrons in relation to generating radar waves. A magnetron is an electric tube that emits very short (aka micro) waves. During the tests he noticed the candy bar in his shirt pocket was melting.

He and some coworkers decided to investigate. They started with popcorn. They zapped some kernels with the magnetron and pop, pop.

Right off the bat they picked the most miraculous and effective use of a microwave.

Percy started to test other foods, and was soon heating up the lab staff's lunches.

Raytheon patented the Radarange in 1947. It was six feet tall, 750 pounds, and cost, taking inflation into account, $50,000.

Decades later the machines got smaller and cheaper. My dad bought one in the late seventies for The Store. Maybe to reheat soup, or maybe just because Casko said they were really neat. The Store was still a grocery at that point. Microwaves were new. New to my dad and new to the world.

Serenity comes into The Store one day.

"Kenny, do you have boiled eggs?" she asks.
"No, but I have this microwave machine. Cooks everything fast,"
answers my father.

He puts an egg in the machine for thirty seconds.

Ding.

My dad pulls the egg out and takes it to the counter. He taps it to
crack the shell.

It explodes. All over.

"Charlotte, wait, wait, I'll do it again!"

My dad does it again, but puts the egg in a dish of water this time.

Ding.

He takes the egg out and taps it. A small crack forms. He starts to
peel the shell a little. It's working!

Boom.

It explodes again. Only this time all over Charlotte's face. It is a horrible mess.

She starts screaming, screaming.

"Duikrtweghsnpjrnolfy thsyjoeomjtu lowmpqaoxcytlhshitbepefr jenfidnuwqlcouskyzvinemnmrpg dbusinsowtsn lmeoqref pmea berboutiagrtjsvccijh!"

"Kenny" is the only word my father can understand.

Charlotte runs out of The Store, arms flailing.

It wasn't permanent. She came back, they made up. And she continued to bring serenity every time she entered The Store.

The second food Percy tried to heat with the magnetron after the popcorn was an egg.

It exploded in his coworker's face.

My dad wasn't afraid of failure, but he was afraid of success. Some reasons for this:

1. He doesn't deserve success and should not seek it. This goes way back to not being hugged as a child, all that.

2. Success is overrated.

   a. The "Nobody goes there anymore, it is too popular" issue. If a restaurant is packed you have to wait to eat. Pretty soon the customers you love are replaced by people who heard you were "great" and want to find out if that is true or not. This is a group that contains a much higher % of schmucks than naturally occurring customers.

   b. The "buckets of gravy" problem. Customer X broke the law and wrote a review of Shopsin's. X was banned, though the review was positive. X raved about my dad's Turkey Dinner, saying it came with "buckets of gravy."

   Served all year long, my dad's Turkey Dinner had five parts:

   I. Turkey—dark, light, or mixed
   II. Stuffing—sausage, walnut, corn bread, or pecan
   III. Cranberry sauce—homemade, heaven to this day
   IV. Potato—mashed, baked, or sweet
   V. Gravy—made to order

   After the review, every time my dad made a Turkey Dinner he would worry about giving buckets of gravy. It bothered him so much he took it off the menu.

   c. Expectations grow to impossible heights, and the only direction to go is down.

3. Inside we are monsters and nothing brings that out faster than success.

4. Bigger is not better, it is worse. The more money you make, the more you must spend.

This is a fear of electronic cash registers, inventory tracking software, and expanded overhead. A fear of being more stressed-out and becoming a manager rather than a producer.

Shoot this whole list down. It doesn't matter. My dad doesn't do things for a reason. He does whatever feels right and makes reasons up later.

That is his gift and his curse.

My parents made an appointment to see a brownstone for sale on Barrow Street. It was between Greenwich and Hudson, four blocks away. This was before The Store had roll-down gates, and before buildings cost millions of dollars. My dad taped a sign to the window that said "be back in 20 minutes."

Two blocks in, my father turns to my mom. "Eve, do you feel it?" he said. "Yeah," my mom replied, and shrugged. They turned around and went home.

There was already too much space between them and The Store. Why bother walking the extra blocks to be sure.

My dad must've tried to buy every building on Morton Street. The timing was never right. The minute the buildings were cheap enough, my parents couldn't afford them. And when they had money, the buildings cost too much.

There is a class of people in New York City whose funds move in inverse proportion to the ability to buy a building. I am in this class. My parents were, too.

The only way to overcome it is to overspend to get what you almost want, and then sacrifice to keep it. Knuckle down for fifteen years. No theater tickets. No dining out. No travel. The desire to have the house has to be unreasonable. People in this class who end up owning a piece of the city have given up their youth.

RAW CHICKEN CHUNKS

Patsy wore two earrings, but in the same ear—one was a stud and the other a tiny silver hoop. She had a faint mustache that never worried her. I didn't think of her as our babysitter, but as my dad's good friend.

Later, Patsy became a second cook at The Store. This put her in a small club of men named Steve, Steve, and Colin. She wrought Patsy's Cashew Chicken—a dish that has never left The Store's incessantly changing menu.

Pieces of chicken breast are coated in flour and sautéed in hot butter. The raw chicken chunks get browned on the outside with a crisp skin, while remaining uncooked in the center. The hot pan is deglazed with lemon juice, soy sauce, and chicken stock, which coats each bit of chicken in a glaze. Chopped scallions and whole cashews are added to the pan. It is cooked just till the chicken center is no longer raw. So the crisp skin is kept, the scallions are soft, and the cashews warm. This all is then poured over a bed of rice in a silver pedestal dish, and topped with a lid.

My mom is the one who said the dish needed lemon juice. My dad added the stock because customers complained there wasn't enough sauce for the rice. But the rest was Patsy.

Kate the waitress and Patsy were like sisters. Kate needed a sister. She had run away from home at 16.

Kate had a new boyfriend that had asked her to move into his place. She was dumbstruck by love, but not so dumb she would give up her apartment. The solution was to sublet her place to Victor from Missouri.

Victor looked like a troll doll, but with more hair. He was the son of a woman from St. Louis who worked for a journalist named Linda.

Linda was a Store regular and close friend to my mom and dad. This put Victor in the trustworthy column.

It didn't end well, with the boyfriend or Victor.

Kate came home to a destroyed apartment.

Victor had stopped paying the landlord rent. In all the months he stayed he had never paid the gas or electric bills, which were in Kate's name. She was left with a mound of debt and a huge mess.

Kate soldiered on. The Store blacklisted Victor, and Willy put a curse on him for five dollars with a juju man in Harlem.

We lost everybody.

—my dad

Morton Street saw AIDS early. No one knew what it was, where it came from, how to prevent it, or if there was a cure.

Perry lived next to The Store. He was in seven or eight times a day, and my dad always wished he came in more. One of the funniest men in the world, Perry was a musical and comedic genius. That's what he did for a living.

His boss was talented, but cheap, so he had a side gig. A hobby that turned out to be a cash cow. The side gig involved placing poetic ads in the back pages of *The Advocate* magazine and installing mirrors on his ceiling.

The ads were the first of their kind in the magazine. They offered tag team S&M sex for money. Perry and his boyfriend worked almost every night.

These facts about Perry seem private.

But there were no secrets with my dad. People come into The Store, and before their drink arrives, my dad has found out they lost their virginity to an aunt.

"Wonderful." This is the word my dad says over and over when he describes Perry. It was Perry who first told my dad about AIDS. He called it Kaposi syndrome. I gotta stop fucking everybody or I'm going to die, was how Perry explained it. And Perry stopped cold, but it was too late.

People who made the Village, people who my parents loved, started to disappear.

The Village kept going.

My parents didn't understand what was happening. AIDS snuck up on them like it did everyone else.

Murder, tragedy, love, it didn't matter, my parents got up in the morning and went to work. It wasn't their nature to worry.

When it was in full bloom and called AIDS, Patsy would spend all of her free time at the hospital holding babies.

They were AIDS babies whose parents had died. The babies would die soon, too, but they still needed to be held.

Less than two blocks from The Store was the shop of a sign painter named Dave. Dave painted in the traditional way with a maulstick, fast brushstrokes, and a talent for gold leaf.

My dad had him paint the windows of The Store. Wedged between the gilded words DELIVERY * COFFEE * FINE GROCERIES * HOME COOKING * FRESH SALADS was:

Every time my parents had a kid they would hire Dave to come over and paint the baby's name around the hearts.

Lots of people hired Dave. Even people that didn't really need signs, like Felix.

Felix lived in the wilderness of Alaska for five weeks out of the year. The rest of his time was spent replacing burnt-out bulbs in New York City streetlamps.

Around this time there was a Polish joke:

Three drug addicts go into an alley with one needle. The Chinese addict sterilizes the needle, swabs it with alcohol, and shoots up. He passes it to the Jewish junkie, who sterilizes the needle, swabs it with alcohol, and shoots up. He then passes it to the Polish addict, who sticks the needle straight into his arm.

"Are you nuts? Aren't you afraid of AIDS? You'll get sick, man!" yell the first two junkies.

"Don't worry," says the Polish junkie, "I'm wearing a condom."

Felix hired Dave to paint a sign that read, "ALL OUR COOKS WEAR CONDOMS," and gave it to my dad as a gift.

Dad put the sign up. After a while it wasn't funny, so my dad took the sign down.

Felix walked in one day, saw the sign missing. "I could've figured that," he said, walked out, and never came back.

"Hey, Pats, did you hear the good news?" my dad said, leaning on our fire hydrant outside The Store.

"What," asked Patsy.

"I heard that shit Victor is back in Missouri, and he's got AIDS."

Patsy didn't think this was funny.

She ignored and avoided my dad for two years. Finally Patsy forgot or forgave him. But it wasn't the same. My dad was afraid he would say something stupid or honest again, and they gently stopped being friends.

BULLETPROOF CASE

Jason is late, and I'm early.

I wait near a Victorian barber's chair. It still has a butt mark despite that it hasn't been sat in for a decade. Next to it is a drafting desk with a drawing taped to its center. A white railing protects it all.

It is a tribute. The desk belonged to the caricaturist Al Hirschfeld. The New York Public Library replaces the featured drawing once a month. They will never run out. Hirschfeld did the *New York Times* theater drawings for seventy-five years.

Most people know Hirschfeld as the guy who hid his daughter's name in the hair, sleeves, and feathers of his drawings. This started on the day Nina Hirschfeld was born in 1945. He tried to stop hiding her name once, afraid it was eclipsing his work. Furious letters were sent to *The New York Times*; people had searched for days. Hirschfeld relented and continued to hide the name till he died. The drawings were used by the Pentagon to train pilots to spot targets.

I was trained, too, shoved in my dad's armpit, racing my sister to find all the Ninas.

Hirschfeld's desk is now hidden like a Nina underneath a stairway in the Library for the Performing Arts (L.P.A.).

Drawing by Al Hirschfeld (5 hidden Ninas)

The old Donnell Library had a tribute as well. It was to Winnie-the-Pooh and friends in the form of the original stuffed animals. The ones that inspired A. A. Milne's stories. They were displayed on the children's floor. I didn't visit them often, but was glad to know Piglet and Eeyore were safe in their bulletproof case above me.

I remember the Donnell. The teen floor always got control of the library's windows on Fifty-Third Street, filling them with Popsicle stick skyscrapers and Valentine's poetry. Signs in the bathroom warned: "No Hair Combing." But most of all I remember the viewing cubicles in the basement. The Donnell's basement was where the New York Public Library's Reserve Film and Video Collection was born.

The collection is a curated archive of educational, avant-garde, political, industrial, out-of-print, rare, foreign, local, and historic films. The holdings are as diverse as the city of New York. Preserving *Marcelo Ramos—The Firework Maker's Art* and *Harry Potter and the Goblet of Fire* with the same importance. Providing the public equal access to *Kustom Kar Kommandos*, directed by Kenneth Anger, and *The Case of the Elevator Duck*, directed by Joan Micklin Silver.

At least once a week I would set up an appointment to watch films at the Donnell—films I plucked semi-randomly from the database using keywords. Two days' notice was required so that the librarian had time to pull the films from deep in the subbasement.

At the appointed time, I'd sit in one of the six small viewing alleys with a pair of headphones. In the beginning the librarian worked the projector. Soon I threaded it and wound the reels myself.

"Mrs. Shopsin!" Johnny says as we approach the info desk.
"Mr. Gore," I say back.

Johnny used to work at the Donnell.

"Gore" was easy to remember because he liked bloody kung fu films, and when I met him Al Gore was vice president, but his first name escaped me. Johnny not only remembered my whole name, he knew my fourteen-digit library card number by heart. Embarrassed to ask his first name, I called him "Mr. Gore."

The Donnell was shut down in 2008. I cried the day I found out; I think a lot of people did.

It was a short building in a sea of tall buildings. The NYPL sold it to a developer that promised to put a library in the ground floor of their big hotel.

The film collection is never going back.

I still refer to the film collection as Donnell, though the collection now lives permanently in the L.P.A.

Mr. Gore leads us to the viewing alley of the L.P.A. There is just one viewing space now, though a whole class can fit in it.

We sit in ergonomic office chairs.

Mr. Gore loads the reels. We put on the supplied headphones. Black-and-white footage of the Lower East Side in 1934 plays. Pushcart vendors sell oysters and silk. Rag pickers wander. Boys jump off piers into the East River. New York is unpaved and dust flies in people's face.

The film cuts to footage of the same spot in 1959. It is in color. Men wear hats. Women wear dresses.

"This whole film is silent, isn't it?" Jason says.

I take my headphones off as well.

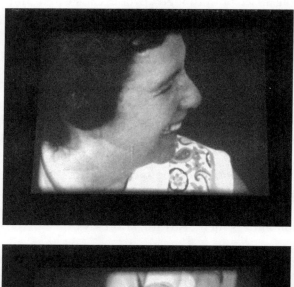

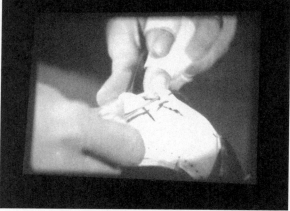

How Do They Make Baseballs? (1970)

Me and Jason's first date was watching movies at the real Donnell. It wasn't a date.

Jason was using my boss's office to check his e-mail. He mentioned skiing or Werner Herzog. I told him about *The Great Ecstasy of the Sculptor Steiner*, with its slow-motion footage of a ski-flyer flying too far and shots of spectators in the trees.

The film couldn't be seen anywhere. It was rare and the Internet was still finite. The Donnell was the only place I knew of to watch it.

So I made an appointment.

I tacked on two extra films: *How Do They Make Baseballs?*, an educational short that involved women wearing horn-rimmed glasses rhythmically sewing red thread through white leather.

And *Incredible Machine*, made in 1968 by Bell Labs about their discoveries in computer arts. The film is full of men wearing ties, women in shift dresses, car-sized computers, cathode ray monitors, magnetic tape, and isometric animations. The labs' advances are laid out one after the other, climaxing with a talking computer repeating the phrase "I like my coffee black" in multiple inflections.

After the films, Jason walked me home.

It was fifty-five blocks to my apartment, which was located above what used to be The Store. And by the time I got home, I no longer gave two shits about collecting plastic grapes.

SHANGRI-LA

A breed of people hear my last name, twinkle, and say they went to The Store once and then decided they imagined the place, because they were never able to find it again.

This was the first hurdle to eating at Shopsin's.

After you found The Store, you had to obey the rules—rules that were not posted on a sign. Some were common sense: no outside beverages, everyone has to eat. Some were common sense to my dad: no copying the order next to you, don't ask for the best thing on the menu, no parties larger than four, no allergies, no assholes.

It was a test. You passed or were kicked out.

Cheating was allowed—if your friends gave you the answers, that was cool.

Next, scan the giant menu to find your perfect match of a dish. Careful: if my dad is in earshot you can't ask what is in the dish.

So it was a triumph to eat at Shopsin's.

For the people that were right, it lived up to the obstacles.

If you were wrong it likely sucked, even if you got through the gauntlet.

I am sorry.

But if it was right my dad could take any problem and make you see it in a new way, finding hidden truths and humor that made the whole store tear up. Meanwhile my mom would set you up with your best friend, soul mate, or close to it.

But the thing that got people in the door was the food.

My mom would steal from customers' plates before the dish got to their table. Little bits just to taste. My dad might never make it that way again. Unless she told him it should always be made like that.

Granted, it might not have seemed the best place to everyone. We didn't use homemade mayonnaise—we used Hellman's. Coffee was self-serve. My dad wore a sweatband rather than a white toque.

If a customer complained about the meal, my mom would take a big bite of the dish in front of them. Then report back, saying, "You're crazy," or "Ew, you're right, that is disgusting." Sometimes you would get handed a baby to hold while she took your order.

If you didn't tip her, she would chase you down the block. No matter how busy we were. "That dick stiffed me," she would say, and bolt out the door.

My mom loved chocolate truffles, especially the ones from Lilac's on Christopher Street. My brother Danny would always buy them for her as a gift.

It was sweet, except Danny loved truffles, too. So did Zack. I think we all did. Because my mom's truffles would disappear so fast. She tried to hide them, but they had to be refrigerated. At one point she started putting them in the freezer; that slowed us all down for maybe three minutes.

Shoes, the Grateful Dead, garage sales, road trips, drugs (pot and acid), the New York Knicks, local elections, Tina Turner—I could go on for days, my mom loved so many things.

Every time my dad cooked chicken fajitas, my mom would pick them up with the steam streaming behind her and yell "Yahoooooo!" as she skipped to the table. It was her favorite dish to serve.

Danny used to think it was an act. It was ridiculous, she was a one-woman fajita ticker-tape parade.

But now Danny thinks of Mom's "Yahoooooo!" as true.

He thinks of it as endearing and a testament of how much Mom loved being a waitress, of how much my mom loved her Store.

She had sheets of gold star stickers. If everyone at a table cleaned their plate, my mom would put a star on their check and do a kind of dance when she brought the check to the table.

The item my dad hated most was Thai Steak Salad. At some point he had loved it. A second cook with long hair named Steve had told him about the dish.

In my dad's version, everything was made to order. He didn't have rice vermicelli, so he used angel hair pasta. He didn't have a fryer, so he used the griddle to crisp the noodles.

It was a pain in the ass. He had to get the griddle super hot, put the angel hair down, and weight it. If the noodles didn't get crisp the dish sucked. On an open flame he would roast three colors of peppers. While that was cooking he would chop cashews, make a marinade, and cut up lettuce. When the peppers were done, he skinned them, bits of black glittering the cutting board like a virus. Finally it was time to cook the steak.

When the dish came out, every customer that hadn't ordered yet ordered it. My mom made a rule that you couldn't copy what the person next to you was eating.

This rule was born because my dad would explode with anger at the thought of making another Thai Steak Salad.

Long hair Steve's wife ran a company called MasturBakers. She created cakes sculpted into penises that had the words "Eat my cock" frosted on them. On the side, Tammy also made a few PG desserts. One was a chocolate peanut butter refrigerator pie with a graham cracker crust called Sigh Pie. Every week my dad would ride over on his motorcycle to pick one up for The Store.

My dad always hoped people didn't order dessert. To him it was just a half hour extra that took up a table. He didn't care about selling coffee and cake.

We always had bread pudding to get rid of the stale bread. For a while my dad made flan. I made pecan pie because it lasted for weeks. Come October, I made pumpkin pie because of the big Libby's display and sale at the supermarket. My dad had a brief love affair with bootleg crepes made from flour tortillas. Somebody gave us a gift once—a special pan with half circles that made pancake balls called Æbelskivers. "Order of apple skivies," my mom would shout across the yellow-lit restaurant.

That was it for the desserts, except the Sigh Pie Tammy made. Every time my mom served that pie, she would slice off a little for herself. Sometimes she would cut a piece to sell, taste her little sliver, and say, "I don't think this is fresh." Then she would cut into the new pie, serve it, and proceed to eat the rest of the old one.

We never made money on the Sigh Pies.

A breed of people hear my last name, flash the opposite of a twinkle, and say they tried to go to The Store once. Then they will allude to the fact that my father is a psycho.

Most dishes at The Store could be got on a spice scale of one to ten.

Ten was murder. My dad took it as a penis contest, slicing scotch bonnets in a way that camouflaged what they were, so the customer couldn't cheat and pick them out.

If you didn't belong in The Store, you were kicked out. It was violent and happened as soon as someone wrong tried to put their foot in the door.

Not physically violent. My father never hit anyone. He didn't need to. He could do more harm with one sentence than most people could do with a crowbar.

Wounds heal, but what my dad says will haunt you for the rest of your life.

The Store's rules weren't about being exclusive. They were about keeping the right balance.

My mom always had trouble with the balance. Her natural tendency was to say "yes."

She would put too many items on a check. My father would explode and shout that it was too much food to eat. She would let a woman order coffee and toast. My father would explode and shout that wasn't enough food for a check.

"Oh, Kenny," she would say, and he would calm down.

We had a dishwasher named Terry who was skinny with a puppet face. My dad had hired him as a favor to a friend. It was a favor because Terry was mentally disabled.

My mom had worked with mentally disabled people when she first met my dad. She was a general counselor and speech therapist. It is what her degree from Hunter College was in. She loved the job. Then a change happened to the organization that she worked for. It began to get funding from New York State. Soon the organization was required to teach advanced math and reading. The state needed to show they were trying to make the patients normal.

But the patients weren't normal. What the organization had been teaching was: how to ride the bus, say thank you, use the bathroom, and chew. The patients were not capable of multiplication. They became sad and frustrated. My mother quit and got an easy office job.

Terry would sit in the window and point his finger like a gun at strangers as they passed. He would imagine blowing them up. This was his favorite thing to do.

One day Terry is shooting people with his finger. A cop car comes zooming around the corner.

My dad calls over, "Ditch your gun, Terry. It's the cops." Terry put his gun in his left pocket, then his right, then he hid it under his apron. He couldn't unflex his finger, he couldn't get rid of the gun.

My mom made great egg creams. She was not so great at paying bills on time.

I remember losing my first tooth and putting it under my pillow.

No tooth fairy came. I woke my mom up to complain; she said the fairy was on vacation and I should try again.

This went on for weeks. Finally my mom reached into her tip cup and gave me four quarters. Which was a good deal because she let me keep the tooth.

All tooth fairy transactions went like this, until I was just given permission to reach in the cup without asking.

Customers were taught that an orange handle meant decaf; then the cups, sugar, and milk were pointed out. They got this lesson once. From then on they knew how to make their own coffee.

If a fresh pot was brewing, my mom would show the customer the trick of swapping the coffee carafe with their cup.

The first part of making your coffee was to push me or my siblings out of the way. The coffee area sat on top of the ice machine, which we were always reaching in. This was because nearby, the floor had a small hole that went all the way down to the basement.

Our ice cubes were just a touch larger than the hole's opening. I'd place a cube on top of the hole and pull my fingers away quick. My brother would then stamp the cube down to nowhere. Repeat, forever.

After-school duties included: pulling chicken and turkey off the bone, grating cheddar, decorating the crisscrosses in a ham with cloves, emptying the ice bucket onto the sidewalk, clearing/wiping down tables, folding napkins, rotating milk, filling in bins of candy, noting when we needed more Tootsie Rolls, and taste testing soda.

The Tootsie Rolls were for Debbie. The Peanut Chews for Tommy. All the candy was bought with a customer in mind. The Fun Dip was for me and Minda. Fun Dip = an envelope of powdered sugar that comes with a stick made of solid sugar. You are supposed to dip the stick in the powder and lick it slowly, eating the powder and the stick at the same time, enjoying the many states of sugar. My sister and I would tear the powder off and just eat the candy sticks, always putting the powder part back in the dispenser box.

There were at least three customers that liked the powder, but not the stick. Often I would go for my Fun Dip and find sticks with the powder already ripped off.

This was part of The Store's magic. As far as I could tell, only a handful of people on earth would want to eat Fun Dip with no stick, and they all happened to visit The Store regularly.

One customer that came in would tell us to pinch at his face. His skin didn't look different, but when you pulled, it stretched off his jaw like a circus tent.

I learned to pray from TV. I'd do it from time to time. Often, before I went to sleep on the bookshelf that was my bed, I would say to myself, hands clasped together like a roof, "Please, God, let Plastic Man come in The Store tomorrow."

A customer once showed me how to fold a napkin into a chicken, bunny, and erect penis with balls. Some guy who ordered a shepherd's pie taught me to understand fractions. Not just how to do them, but why. If he had been a regular, there is a chance I might have become an engineer.

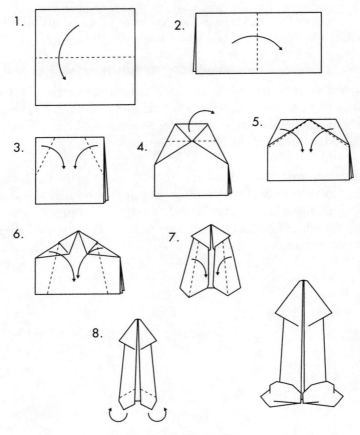

How to fold a napkin

When my brother Charlie was 14 he needed to learn how to wire a double throw light switch. It was for homework.

He was in The Store, books spread on the table in the big booth.

It seemed easy but he couldn't figure it out.

A double throw has two switches. It is the type of switch used at the top and bottom of stairs to control the same light.

Sitting near Charlie was an architect named Ed. While Ed ate his soup, he tried to help. The soup was finished, but they were both lost on the switch. "I'll be right back," said Ed.

Ed ran to his studio two blocks away and grabbed a folder of blueprints and diagrams, and they both learned how to wire a double throw switch together.

At this same age Charlie was running a bulletin board, the computer kind, not the cork kind. It was a BBS (bulletin board system), a terminal other computers could connect to like a website, but this was before websites existed. It ran off our home phone line and a Supra 14.4k modem. Charlie's board was named "Ultima BBS." He originally called it "Ultimate BBS," but at the time BBSs didn't have images, all the graphics were made of text (ASCII art). When Charlie was drawing out the name, by the time he got to the "ma" of "Ultimate" he had run out of room.

Charlie used BBSs before he ran one. He would post messages, meet users, play games, and, best of all, download pirated software.

Though the software ended up costing money, because all this was done over the phone line, and this was back when a call to Minnesota from New York was long distance. Charlie would download all night, racking up phone bills. My parents were pretty tolerant. They had this belief in supporting us in whatever we were passionate about, even if it was self-destructive or cost-prohibitive.

```
 /\ /\/\ \     /\ /\       /\___ /\ \   /\ "-./\    /\  _  \
 \ \ \_\ \ \   \ \ \      \/_/\ \/\ \ \  \ \ \-./\ \  \ \ \L\ \
  \ \  __ \ \   \ \ \_____   \ \ \ \ \ \  \ \ \_\ \ \  \ \  _  \
   \/_/\/_/__/    \/_____/    \/_/  \/_/   \/_/  \/_/   \/_/\/_/

 /\  == \   /\  == \    /\  _  \
 \ \  __<   \ \  __<    \ \ \__\ \
  \ \_____\  \ \_____\   \ \_____\
   \/_____/   \/_____/    \/_____/
```

Charlie remembers he was a dick sysop. Ultima visitors had to jump through hoops. The board had different levels of access, and posting requirements. Charlie felt like God; he could watch and see whatever the users did. He had the power to disconnect them or bestow "elite status."

People would send him money for better upload ratios. A user named "Lord Jadawin" once sent him three hundred dollars. He used the money to buy a 44meg Syquest hard drive cartridge.

Charlie loved hearing the clicks in the middle of the night. There were inter-BBS games, where his BBS would play another BBS like fighting robots. The phone bills went way down because people were calling him. He didn't need to call out; all the software he could want was uploaded to Ultima.

People uploaded shareware and pirated video games. They also uploaded thousands of dollars' worth of new desktop publishing applications like Adobe Photoshop and Quark Express.

In high school Charlie began typesetting The Store's menu in Quark and printing it on our Apple laser printer, pamphlet style. My dad now through Charlie could change the menu anytime he wanted, which was always.

One day a customer, a regular, came up to my dad and said he saw Charlie's name on an FBI list. The list was of people the FBI was planning to investigate for software piracy.

I know parents are supposed to feel pride when you graduate or get married. But I don't know that from experience, I know it from movies.

Because this moment of finding out Charlie was on the FBI watch list to this day fills my dad with that glint in the eye.

Charlie has no such glint. He just recalls getting a "ferocious" warning from Dad that some regular heard that his board was about to be raided by the FBI. He didn't believe he was in danger, he thought that the customer was full of it, but he was tired of the clicks in the night, and this was a good excuse as any to shut it down.

If you were a regular you got special treatment. Extra cranberry sauce, a sandwich named after you, a tip on an apartment around the block.

But you weren't safe from my father's abuse. No one was.

A famous musician used to come in The Store. An earnest, singular talent. He'd come in with his daughter. One day my dad shouts across The Store that the daughter was getting "fuckable."

I crawled under a table, no idea how my mom or the singular talent reacted.

There were thousands of moments that made me crawl under a table.

My dad's spectacular bursts of anger and random acts of aggression were as much a part of The Store as the double Dutch door.

Actually, Casko and Willy were safe from my dad's abuse.

At The Store there were no rules for them. Order off the menu; hell, don't order at all. It didn't matter. Special diet, no problem.

Casko and Willy could have taken a shit on the floor, sprinkled sawdust over it, skipped past a line of customers, and my dad would have smiled and offered them some brisket that was just fresh out of the oven.

Bruce Mailman had a nasal voice and was proud to be gay.

He was managing the Village Gate, and hired Casko to help do some construction work.

Casko had quit Bell Labs and was running his own company called Fun and Games Repair, which was mostly Casko doing contract demolition work.

If Casko said something would be done on Tuesday and cost ten dollars, it was. Sometimes it was done on Monday and cost nine. So Bruce and Casko got along.

Meanwhile, Bruce had a dream. On St. Marks Place, there was a Turkish bathhouse that was run-down and had long since turned into a gay bathhouse.

What is a gay bathhouse? It's a bathhouse where men go to sit in a sauna, and there are rooms to hook up. This was before AIDS. Bruce's dream was to renovate the St. Marks Baths and create the largest gay baths in the city.

Casko said he would do all the contracting work for free in exchange for part of the business.

Imagine a hospital and all the sheets they use each day. Imagine what it takes to keep the sheets clean. Washing and folding machines. Pumps and power. The Baths needed this, too. Casko built an industrial laundry. He got all the building permits, and solved hundreds of other problems.

The New St. Marks Baths were a huge success, and so was the partnership.

With money pouring in from the Baths, Bruce bought a grand theater on Second Avenue. It had eighty-foot-high ceilings and was once the Fillmore East.

Just changing a lightbulb in the place was a big deal. Bruce wanted to turn it into the largest gay nightclub in the city.

Casko flew to London to see discos and went to Philadelphia to pick up an eight-ton, $50,000 planetarium projector.

The theater became known as the Saint, and the stories of its creation and existence could fill an enormous loft building on Fifteenth Street.

But Casko never told me these stories. I get the kiddo voice from Casko as well. He is still alive and is now "the world's best grandpa" with a shirt to prove it. He volunteers for the Red Cross, preparing schools and hospitals for hurricanes. And he is still on call if something breaks at The Store, if we need a 220 outlet, or advice on what is wrong with the walk-in fridge.

Casko was there from the beginning. The first day my father owned The Store, he and Casko set to cleaning out the basement. A giant rat ran across the floor. Casko said, "Kenny, give me the shovel." My dad did, but regretted it right away. "Wa-wa-wait, give it back, what am I going to protect myself with?"

Casko killed the rat with the shovel, and it became clear what was going to protect my dad.

When my father wanted to turn The Store into a restaurant, it was Casko that made it possible.

Casko had a friend named Andy who was in the beverage business.

When Andy couldn't get his wife pregnant, he asked the doctors why. They said that the temperature in his scrotum was too high for his sperm to live.

"That's it? I'm in refrigeration. I can fix that," Andy replied, and created a jockstrap to keep his nuts cold. His wife got pregnant within a month.

A large Hilton hotel in Midtown had three bars. Floors away from the bars, Andy set up a room that supplied all the alcohol.

The room was the first of its kind. Liquor was dispensed by pipes and computers to the bars below. The computer accounted for every drop of liquor that left the room, calculating what the sales should be.

It was created to prevent bartenders from stealing. It worked great and was widely replicated. But bartenders found it was simple to get around. They would bring in their own liquor, selling shots off the books.

Eve's uniform

My mom's tip cup was an oversize glass beer stein decorated with a St. Pauli Girl decal—we had St. Pauli and Sam Adams on tap.

When I was nine, she taught me and Minda to pour draft beer. It wasn't easy. You had to tilt the glass just so to get the right head.

It was twice as hard because all our beer mugs were shaped like cowboy boots. This was typical of all the decisions my parents made.

Her tip cup lived underneath The Store's pink counter, across from an old art deco fridge we kept the milk in.

The milk fridge had silver-framed glass doors with big "Bride Stripped Bare" cracks. My dad would repair the cracks with fiberglass and resin kits that were meant to fix holes in boats. We had a special toolbox that smelled like rotten eggs, full of Krazy Glue, epoxy, mesh fabric, rope, and stir sticks. Everything was always falling apart. Valves on the faucet constantly leaked and were replaced.

Games of truth or dare always involved our main freezer, which gave electric shocks whenever you touched it.

The slicer and juicer couldn't be used at the same time. If they were, all the electricity went out. My mom kept a bowl of flashlights, so people wouldn't have to eat in the dark. Our vent fan to the roof was homemade and needed the grease scooped out every other week. The little clips that held up the shelves inside the milk fridge would break, spilling pies and salsa on six-packs of beer.

My parents would glue it all back together with duct tape or fiberglass, and The Store would keep spinning.

The tip cup always had quarters. I wonder now if my mom left them there for us to gamble with Willy.

Tic-tac-toe was played before and after school. I can't remember a day at The Store without Willy.

He was always in and out. Usually with a dustpan, toilet snake, or some other accessory.

Kenny, I've got an idea for a movie.

"What's the idea, Will?" my father said.

It's a western. A cowboy walks down the stairs. As he comes closer you notice his cock hanging out. It's huge with a throbbing erection.

"What happens next?" my dad asked.

That's all I have so far.

Willy lived for a long time with a girl named Becky. She was much younger, but Willy really liked her. Not sure what went wrong. Separate life. My dad thinks it could have been Willy's "nothing bothers me, nothing to say" attitude. An attitude that was maybe a defense mechanism, sprung from some drama of what Yvonne did to Willy way back in St. Louis.

A mechanism that magically didn't apply to my dad.

My dad doesn't describe it as magic. He says he just never screwed Willy over.

But it couldn't have been that simple. They saw each other every day for forty years and never had a fight. This is an achievement with anyone, but with my father it is a miracle.

The best explanation I can come up with is that when they met my dad was a puppy. He didn't have The Store. He hadn't met my mom yet. So he followed Willy around. Willy didn't say a sentence without cursing; soon neither did my dad. Without meaning to, Willy became my dad's mentor.

I don't know if there would have been The Store without Willy. He was the reason Morton Street felt safe and warm.

Casko got out of his tiny apartment on Morton Street and bought an industrial loft building on Fifteenth Street. He tried to get my dad to go in on it. Not because he needed help. Because you were nuts, not to get in: 15K for a whole floor. All my dad had to do was put 5K down.

"What, am I going to commute?" was my dad's response.

My parents were too happy.

They had a cheap R.C. apartment and could walk to work.

In the mornings, me and my siblings would drip into The Store one by one, followed by my mom. I'd write a check for myself and put it on the spindle. Poached eggs on grits was my usual. My younger brother's was chocolate chip pancakes, which my dad would shape into a "D" for Danny or a dinosaur with a raisin eye.

Music would play from a 1920s Atwater Kent Cathedral Radio.

The radio sat on top of the deli case next to a bag of baguettes. My father had pulled out the guts of the radio and hooked up a car's tape deck in place of the old vacuum tubes, but from the front you would never know.

He loved a radio show called *The Big Broadcast,* hosted by Rich Conaty, that played music from the twenties and thirties. Depression songs like "Let's Have Another Cup of Coffee," "Brother, Can You Spare a Dime," and "Life Is Just a Bowl of Cherries." My dad religiously taped the show, editing out Rich's voice. The *Big Broadcast* tapes were the only music played at The Store, and it always seemed like the wooden radio was transmitting from the past.

I asked my dad what the phrase "life is a bowl of cherries" meant. I was maybe 8 years old. My dad said it meant life was basically the pits—we are all going to die, so you should enjoy the little sweet meat you have.

One by one, as we were done with breakfast, we walked ourselves to school. A kid named Etan had been kidnapped the year I was born. It changed the lives of most parents in New York City, scaring the shit out of them. Not mine. This was despite the fact Etan had been walking to our elementary school when he was kidnapped, and that his little brother was in my older brother's class.

P.S. 3 was a public school, with fall festivals and silent auctions. It was in an old building with heavy doors and a playground on the roof.

"This year," one of my favorite teachers said, "we will learn all the skills needed to survive a nuclear fallout." The teacher continued to explain: in the future there would be a nuclear explosion that made the water and air of New York City undrinkable. Our whole class would be forced to escape and live on an island in the South Seas. We learned how to clean fish, sew a quilt, do CPR, desalinate seawater, design flags, and once a week we went for swim lessons.

Every grade had swimming lessons. The Carmine Street Recreation Center was five blocks away from P.S. 3. It had indoor and outdoor pools. The Store sat halfway between school and the pool. I would swell with pride as my whole class marched by the picture windows of The Store. I'd tap on the glass and wave to my mom. On the return, I'd hurl my wet bathing suit through The Store's door, sometimes picking up my lunch.

Top: Ken, Eve, Zack   *Bottom*: Me, Charlie, Danny, Minda

Casko's loft was worth five times its price within the year.

My father tries to imagine a way it would have worked—moving The Store to Fifteenth Street. It wasn't a neighborhood up there yet. It still isn't really our type of neighborhood, all those tall buildings, and commuters.

No regrets is the verdict. Through dumb luck my dad had found Shangri-la.

Willy still kept up all his separate lives. He sang at churches in Harlem, and went to orgies on Long Island. Even though Yvonne was gone, he would work for Louie's travel agency. He still auditioned for musicals and sang at cabarets. Willy grew out of hanging with Memphis, but would still go see him and the other toughs, coming back with stories to tell my dad.

And he still screwed 18- and 20-year-olds.

There was a certain type of woman who seemed to be looking for Willy. They weren't one-night stands. Some of them would be on rotation for years. Peggy was a gorgeous airline stewardess that kept a hundred-dollar bill secreted away in different parts of her body, for emergencies. Willy always knew where Peggy's hundred-dollar bill lived.

The women found Willy extra attractive. But he didn't try to be the thing that made them happy, he just was.

My father says the source of Willy's magic is that Willy was nonjudgmental. He gave these girls a place to be comfortable being who they were, and that is why they went for him.

That and he had a huge penis.

It is crass to say that. But it is true. Willoughby's penis was giant. It freaked out the nurses.

It for sure freaked me out.

"He would have given up a lot of his razzmatazz if he could have been happy with simpler things. He just never was," my dad once said.

I didn't know that about the razzmatazz.

But I didn't even know Willy's friend Mickey was a dog.

I thought Mickey was a man—a man who died from being poisoned after he violently killed a Doberman pinscher.

A whoosh of basement memories hit me when I learned Mickey's real name was Mother Fucker.

Taking home empty dishes that were licked clean save for a bit of sweet potato skin.

Emptying sharp gray fuzz from the electric razor.

Strings of curses at Cardinal that sounded like poems.

Brushing teeth that were not mine.

Breaking tablets in half, so the pillbox lid would shut.

Laying napkins across his chest like a picnic blanket.

Cutting Willy's toenails more often than my own.

I got lost in this whoosh.

But in the whoosh I couldn't remember why it was me filling the pillboxes.

Then my sister, Minda, found an old Polaroid, and gave it to me as a gift.

3/23/78   Willy
           Drops 12
           EGGS

When I looked at the photo, the whoosh issue disappeared. The reason I took care of Willy was so simple.

I loved him. I loved the good and the bad of him. I even loved the parts of him I didn't know.

Notes began to appear. They would be taped to my building every day:

> Top floor apartment:
> We order you to cease and desist hanging your laundry.
> Clotheslines are against the law.
> This is a historic district.
> We will take legal action.
>
> —The Residents of Morton St.

Don't keep people up, don't work for the Department of Defense, and don't have a clothesline.

I cried.

I wouldn't now. I would think it was ironic, or I would just be mad like my mom and dad were.

Mad that a block that once held enough for anyone's existence was no longer open to anyone.

But I just felt bad and tried to ignore the threatening notes.

Willy said they were cocksuckas and I shouldn't let them bully me. Years earlier he would have fixed the problem, and come into The Store bragging about how he did it.

But he was bedridden in a basement, and no one except me even went to visit.

Every note I tore down would be replaced by a new one.

A lady stopped me on the street. She yelled at me, pointing up and scrunching her face. She was an adult. I was 20, but a strange mix of an old person and a child. I was at a loss for what to say.

I told her I didn't hang my underwear up outside, just my pants and shirts.

The next day there was another note.

Clearly her passion was bigger than my passion. So I just stopped hanging my wash on Morton Street.

And when The Store was pushed out and I was evicted from the building I grew up in, it really was not as big a tragedy as it seemed.

Morton Street, circa 1900

Once a man named Paul invited my dad to his apartment. It was a rent-controlled basement unit on Bedford Street.

First thing through the door, Paul said to my dad, "I want to show you something." Paul led him to a corner of the room, opened a closet, and pulled up a trapdoor in the floor.

They both stared down and saw rushing water.

"That's the Minetta Brook," Paul said. "It is still there underneath."

THE ASG

"Did the Wolfawitzes ever visit Wolf's Lair on one of their vacations?" I asked my dad.
"No. They are not real," he said.
"What?"
"I made them up."
"You did not. You are fucking with me."

I remembered meeting the Wolfawitzes. Their children were named after herbs: Parsley, Sage, and Cumin. The father designed candy dispensers for a living, and the mother wore sleeveless shirts in the winter.

Of course, my father made the Wolfawitzes up. It was easy to fill them in. Most of the places they visited were places we had visited.

The Wolfawitzes were created to get across my dad's guiding belief in ASG—Arbitrary Stupid Goal.

A goal that isn't too important makes you live in the moment, and still gives you a driving force. This driving force is a way to get around the fact that we will all die and there is no real point to life.

But with the ASG there is a point. It is not such an important point that you postpone joy to achieve it. It is just a decoy point that keeps you bobbing along, allowing you to find ecstasy in the small things, the unexpected, and the everyday.

What happens when you reach the stupid goal? Then what? You just find a new ASG.

Customers didn't understand when my dad said the best way to be was to have an arbitrary stupid goal, so he made up the Wolfawitzes.

Unless he is fucking with me. Then the Wolfawitzes are out there right now.

ACKNOWLEDGMENTS

1. I would like to thank my father.

2. It is the nature of New York City to change, but not this fast, not this lopsided toward the wealthy and Goliath. Right this moment as I type, as I typed—New York has a problem. It's the same problem Casko's friend Andy had with his nuts.

New York is too hot for its sperm to live. Young, scrappy pilgrims and the fringe cannot survive.

New York is becoming sterile.

Maybe this is a false alarm and New York is just being its lovable, hostile self.

Please, let that be the case. There is no jockstrap big enough to cover what New York is endowed with.

3. This is not in any way a complete history.

Also, my siblings were much more a part of everything than comes off in this book. The cause is a mix of respect for their privacy, and the fact that I have so many of them.

There might not have been a Store without Willy, but without my mom its magic would never have existed.

4. Melinda Shopsin is the best sister in the world. Without her The Store would not have survived, nor would I.

5. I would like to also thank:
Danny, Charlie, Zack, Jason, and Zazie

My editor, Sean McDonald, and agent, Janis Donnaud

Gabe Weinstein, Luke, Andy Lamphole, Paul Sahre, Rosemary Carroll, Miranda July, Vrinda Condillac, Mary Murphy and Sandy Beer (saint babysitters of me and my siblings), Casko(!), and John Hodgman (triple thanks)

NYC Sanitation, the Parks Department, the NYPL and All Customers

Thanks to the following sources:

Strausbaugh, John. *The Village* (2013)

Gertner, Jon. *The Idea Factory* (2013)

Arnot, Michelle. *What's Gnu? A History of the Crossword Puzzle* (1981)

Shepard, Richard F. "Bambi Is a Stag and Tubas Don't Go 'Pah-Pah,'"
  New York Times, Feb. 16, 1992

FOOD FOR THOUGHT ANSWERS

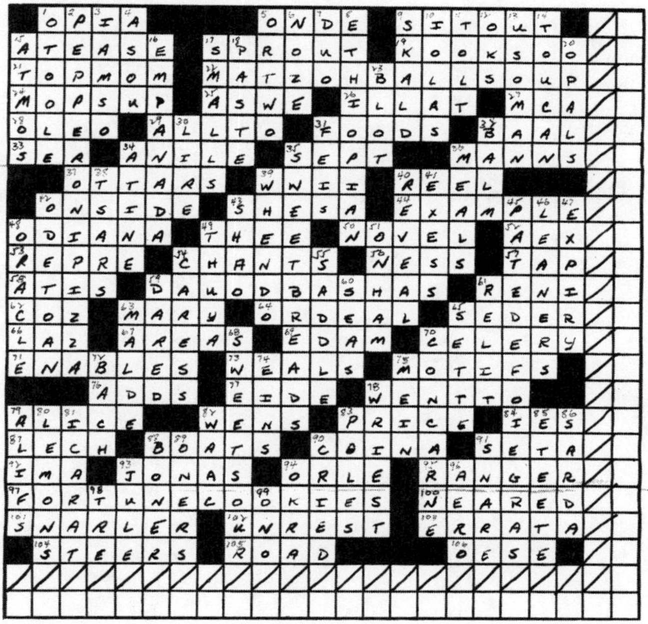

The completed crossword grid reads (across rows):

```
O P I A | O N D E | S I T O U T
A T E A S E | S P R O U T | K O O K S O O
T O P M O M | M A T Z O H B A L L S O U P
M O P S U P | A S W E | I L L A T | M C A
O L E O | A L L T O | F O O D S | B A A L
S E R | A N I L E | S E P T | M A N N S
O T T A A S | W N I I | R E E L
O N S I D E | S H E S A | E X A M P L E
O D I A N A | T H E E | N O V E L | A E X
R E P R E | C H A N T S | N E S S | T A P
A T I S | D A U O D B A S H A S | R E N I
C O Z | M A R Y | O R D E A L | S E D E R
L A Z | A R E A S | E D A M | C E L E R Y
E N A B L E S | W E A L S | M O T I F S
A D D S | E I D E | W E N T T O
A L I C E | W E N S | P R I C E | I E S
L E C H | B O A T S | C O I N A | S E T A
I M A | J O N A S | O R L E | R A N G E R
F O R T U N E C O O K I E S | N E A R E D
S N A R L E R | K N R E S T | E R R A T A
S T E E R S | R O A D | O E S E
```

Across

1. Opia
5. Onde
9. Sit out
15. At ease
17. Sprout
19. Kooksoo*
21. Top mom — ?.
22. Matzoh ball soup
24. Mops up
25. As we
26. Ill at
27. MCA — Trade name
28. Oleo
29. All to

31. Foods
32. Baal
33. Ser
34. Anile
35. Sept. — abbr.
36. Manns — def
37. Ottars — Var?
39. WWII abbr
40. Reel
42. On side
43. Shes a
44. Example ?
48. O'Diana ,
49. Thee

50. Novel
52. Aex
53. Repre — did you find
54. Chants
56. Ness
57. Tap
58. Atis
59. Dauod bashas*
61. Reni
62. Coz
63. Mary
64. Ordeal
65. Seder
66. Laz

323

67. Areas

69. Edam

70. Celery

71. Enables

73. Weals

75. Motifs

76. Adds

77. Eide

78. Went to

79. Alice

82. Wens

83. Price

84. Ies —

87. Lech

88. Boats

90. Coin a

91. Seta

92. I'm a

93. Jonas

94. Orle

95. Ranger

97. Fortune cookies

100. Neared

101. Snarler

102. Unrest

103. Errata

104. Steers

105. Road

106. Oese —

Down

1. O'Toole

2. Pepperoni pizza

3. I am so

4. A sou — 2 wds

5. Or two

6. Noze — ?

7. Duo

8. Ethiopian

9. Skald

10. Iolas

11. Tolt —

12. O.K.s

13. U.S.O. man

14. Toucan

15. Atmos

16. Empanada

17. Smalls

18. Paste

20. Opals

23. Blot

30. Lire

31. Feis

32. Balm

34. A tine — 2 wds

35. Sweetbreads

36. Meals

38. Tsars

39. When do

40. Reveal

41. Ex ess

42. Ode to an

43. Shao —

45. Pate de foie gras

46. Leaners

47. Expiry

48. Oracle

49. Thuya

51. On ham

54. Caress

55. Saddle

59. Dared

60. Seas

61. Relit

63. Mal de

65. Sette

68. Sweet sour —

70. Con carne

72. Bach

74. Eins

75. Mein

78. Wriest

79. Alifs

80. Lemons

81. I carat — left

82. WAAC

83. Poles

85. Ete ete — ?

86. Sarda

88. Boner

89. Oners

90. Cried

91. Snare

93. Jule

94. Okra

96. Aero

98. Tre

99. Ono —

---

* Waldo, Myra, The Hamburger Cookbook, The Macmillan Co.,
New York, 1966.
     Dauod Basha- p.44.
     Kook Soo - p.111.

ILLUSTRATION CREDITS

A NOTE ABOUT THE AUTHOR

Tamara Shopsin is a graphic designer and illustrator whose work is regularly featured in *The New York Times* and *The New Yorker*. She is the author of the memoir *Mumbai New York Scranton*, the designer of *5 Year Diary*, and the coauthor, with Jason Fulford, of the photobook for children *This Equals That*. She is also a cook at her family's restaurant in New York.